Home Preserving

CAVENDISH HOUSE

CONTENTS

Editor: Renny Harrop
Art Editor: Judith Robertson
Illustrator: Caroline Austin

Published by
Marshall Cavendish Books Limited
58 Old Compton Street
LONDON W1V 5PA

© Marshall Cavendish Limited 1976, 1981, 1982

First printing 1976 (softback)
Second printing 1981 (hardback)
Third printing 1982 (hardback)

ISBN 0 85685 961 3
Printed and bound by
Encuadernaciones Belgas, S.L., Bilbao, Spain

Editor's Note: American terminology is indicated
throughout the text by ( ) brackets,
e.g. 600ml/1 pint (2½ cups)

Add the pears to the syrup and simmer for 5 to 10 minutes, or until tender – but not mushy. Using a slotted spoon, lift the pears from the pan and place them in a wide-necked sterilized jar.

Continue to simmer the syrup for a further 5 minutes, then measure it and add 600ml/1 pint (2½ cups) to the brandy. Stir to mix well, then pour over the pears and seal the jar. Leave for one month, or longer, before opening.

Fruit preserved in this way will keep for several months if unopened and for approximately 10 days once the jar is unsealed, provided that the fruit remains fully immersed in the liquid.

Variations

Other fruits, such as peaches and strawberries can be preserved in the same way, but the softer the fruit the shorter the cooking time it will require. The inclusion of brandy is not essential. A quantity of extra syrup can be used instead and the results will be very delicious.

Blackberry Liqueur

	Metric/UK	US
Blackberry juice	2½l/4pts	5pts
Sugar	900g/2lb	4 cups
Grated nutmeg	4tbsp	4tbsp
Whole cloves	2tbsp	2tbsp
Brandy	400ml/ 15fl oz	2 cups

Place the blackberry juice and sugar in a preserving pan or large saucepan. Bring to the boil and if necessary remove the scum from the top.

Add the nutmeg and cloves and simmer for 15 minutes. Remove from the heat and add the brandy.

Pour into a crock or jug and cover the top tightly. Set aside for 3 days.

Sterilize and dry 2 or 3 bottles.

Strain the liqueur through a piece of muslin or cheesecloth, placed over a jug or mixing bowl. Pour the liqueur into the bottles and seal with new corks.

Allow at least 1 month for the liqueur to mature before serving.

Brandied Cherries

About 1kg (2lb)	Metric/UK	US
Cherries	1kg/2lb	2lb
Sugar	1½kg/3lb	6 cups
Water	1¼l/2pts	5 cups
Brandy		

Remove the stalks from the cherries and wash in cold water. In a large saucepan dissolve 450g/1lb (2 cups) of sugar in the water over moderate heat. Bring the syrup to the boil, skimming off any froth which may rise to the surface.

Brandied Cherries and Pears in Brandy are two mouth-watering ways of preserving fruit.

General information

INDEX

Picture credits:

Rex Bamber 39;
Barnaby's 9;
Steve Bicknell 52L; 53; 55R;
Michael Boys 32;
Camera Press 54;
Alan Duns 11; 15; 18; 21T; 34; 37; 47; 50; 51; 55L;
V. Finnis 27; 33;
Brian Furner 12B;
Melvin Grey 6; 35; 43; 56; 57; 58; 62/3;
J. Hovell 38;
George E. Hyde 14; 17; 23B;

David Levin 2;
Max Logan 30;
David Meldrum 5; 42;
Roger Phillips 1; 8; 10; 12T; 16; 19; 21B; 22; 23T; 26; 28; 44;
   48/9; 50B; 60; 61; 64;
Iain Reid 46;
David Smith 4; 7; 20; 31; 40/1;
H. Smith 36; 52R;
Syndication International 13;
Transworld 29;
Jerry Tubby 24;

Add the pears to the syrup and simmer for 5 to 10 minutes, or until tender – but not mushy. Using a slotted spoon, lift the pears from the pan and place them in a wide-necked sterilized jar.

Continue to simmer the syrup for a further 5 minutes, then measure it and add 600ml/1 pint (2½ cups) to the brandy. Stir to mix well, then pour over the pears and seal the jar. Leave for one month, or longer, before opening.

Fruit preserved in this way will keep for several months if unopened and for approximately 10 days once the jar is unsealed, provided that the fruit remains fully immersed in the liquid.

Variations

Other fruits, such as peaches and strawberries can be preserved in the same way, but the softer the fruit the shorter the cooking time it will require. The inclusion of brandy is not essential. A quantity of extra syrup can be used instead and the results will be very delicious.

Blackberry Liqueur

	Metric/UK	US
Blackberry juice	2½l/4pts	5pts
Sugar	900g/2lb	4 cups
Grated nutmeg	4tbsp	4tbsp
Whole cloves	2tbsp	2tbsp
Brandy	400ml/ 15fl oz	2 cups

Place the blackberry juice and sugar in a preserving pan or large saucepan. Bring to the boil and if necessary remove the scum from the top.

Add the nutmeg and cloves and simmer for 15 minutes. Remove from the heat and add the brandy.

Pour into a crock or jug and cover the top tightly. Set aside for 3 days.

Sterilize and dry 2 or 3 bottles.

Strain the liqueur through a piece of muslin or cheese-cloth, placed over a jug or mixing bowl. Pour the liqueur into the bottles and seal with new corks.

Allow at least 1 month for the liqueur to mature before serving.

Brandied Cherries

About 1kg (2lb)	Metric/UK	US
Cherries	1kg/2lb	2lb
Sugar	1½kg/3lb	6 cups
Water	1¼l/2pts	5 cups
Brandy		

Remove the stalks from the cherries and wash in cold water. In a large saucepan dissolve 450g/1lb (2 cups) of sugar in the water over moderate heat. Bring the syrup to the boil, skimming off any froth which may rise to the surface.

Brandied Cherries and Pears in Brandy are two mouth-watering ways of preserving fruit.

When the syrup is clear, add the cherries, a few at a time, and boil for 1 minute. Remove the cherries from the pan with a slotted spoon and set them aside on a plate to cool.

Measure 600ml/1 pint (2½ cups) of the syrup and put it in a pan with the remaining sugar.

Place the pan over low heat and allow the sugar to dissolve slowly. When the sugar is completely dissolved raise the heat and boil rapidly, removing any scum with a metal spoon.

Continue boiling until the syrup is clear or reaches 110°C (213°F) on a sugar (candy) thermometer.

Remove the pan from the heat and leave to cool slightly. Then strain the syrup through a clean cloth into a jug.

Measure the strained syrup, add an equal quantity of brandy and stir well.

Pack the cherries into the jars and pour the syrup over them, ensuring that the cherries are covered.

Seal the jars and leave them in a cool, dry place for at least 4 to 6 months.

Peach Brandy

	Metric/UK	US
Fresh peaches. sliced and stones (pits) reserved	½kg/1lb	1lb
Sugar	225g/8oz	1 cup
Brandy	475ml/ 16fl oz	2 cups
Grated nutmeg	½tsp	½tsp

Place the peach slices in a mixing bowl. Add the sugar, brandy and nutmeg and stir well to mix. Crack the peach stones (pits) and remove the inside kernels. Remove the skin and add the kernels to the peach mixture.

Pour into a crock or jug and cover the top tightly. Set aside for 1 to 2 weeks to infuse.

Sterilize and dry 1 or 2 bottles.

Strain the liqueur through a piece of muslin or cheese-cloth placed over a jug or mixing bowl, squeeze as much liquid out as possible. Pour the liquid into the bottles and seal with new corks.

Allow at least one month for the liqueur to mature before serving.

Peaches in Brandy

About 1½kg (3lb)	Metric/UK	US
Small peaches	1kg/2lb	2lb
Sugar	1½kg/3lb	6 cups
Water	1¼l/2pts	5 cups
Brandy	600ml/1pt	2½ cups

Place the peaches in a large heatproof mixing bowl and pour over enough boiling water to cover them com-

Enjoy the flavour of Peaches in Brandy, regardless of season, either on their own or made up into a delicious and intoxicating fruit fool and delight your dinner guests.

pletely. Set aside for 3 minutes.

With a slotted spoon, remove the peaches from the bowl. Discard the water. Skin the peaches, cut them in half and remove and discard the stones (pits).

In a large saucepan, dissolve the sugar in the water over low heat, stirring constantly. Increase the heat to moderate and bring the syrup to the boil. Carefully lower the peach halves into the syrup and poach them for 1 minute.

Remove the pan from the heat. Using a slotted spoon, lift the peaches out of the syrup and place them in clean, dry preserving jars, filling the jars three-quarters full. Set aside.

Pour 600ml/1 pint (2½ cups) of the syrup into a medium-sized saucepan. Discard the remaining syrup. Place the pan over moderately high heat and bring the syrup to the boil, stirring occasionally. Boil the syrup, without stirring, until it registers 110°C (220°F) on a sugar (candy) thermometer, or until a teaspoon of the syrup dropped into cold water forms a soft ball when rolled between your fingertips.

Remove the pan from the heat and stir in the brandy. Combine the mixture thoroughly and pour it over the peaches in the preserving jars.

Seal the jars with their vacuum lids and store them in a cool, dry dark place for at least 4 months before using.

Preserving is one of the most satisfying activities that can be carried out in your own home. Although the introduction of convenience foods, particularly of the frozen variety, meant that, for a while, home-preserving became almost a lost art, it is now enjoying a revival.

The original objective of storing away food in times of plenty to supplement provisions when food became scarce has only been slightly modified. Today we preserve food because it is the best way of making use of surplus crops, whether bought, cultivated or gathered free, before time and chemistry cause them to deteriorate.

The principal causes of deterioration are the uncontrolled growth of micro-organisms, enzyme activity, oxidation and dehydration. The type and rate of deterioration vary from one kind of food to another and also on storage conditions. Therefore, the primary rule to follow for effective preserving is to use food that is fresh, of good quality, and clean.

If fresh food can be obtained at its prime, there are countless ways of preserving it so that it retains most of its nutritional value. It may change slightly in texture and taste in the processing, but the results will be delicious, useful and money-saving. Because this book is designed for people who want to produce consistently good quality preserves with as little time and effort as possible, only those methods are included which require the minimum of equipment and expertise. However, it is advisable to read the introduction to each section before progressing to the recipes as this will avoid any expensive mistakes.

Of course, preserves are available commercially, many of which are excellent. They are, however, often expensive and do not compare for flavour with those made in your own home. Discover for yourself the pleasure of eating a spicy chutney or tempting jam that you have made yourself by following the information given in this book, and at the same time, build up a store of provisions that will not only be of convenience to yourself but make excellent and acceptable presents.

I

Jams, jellies & marmalades

The making of jams, jellies and marmalades is one of the most popular ways of preserving fruit. Although the methods used in their preparation vary, the basic principles are the same.

Equipment

A preserving pan This should be made of aluminium, stainless steel or unchipped enamel. If using a metal pan, do not allow fruit to stand in it longer than is necessary. Choose a pan that is both large and wide. The pan should never be more than two-thirds full at any stage in the proceedings.

Jam jars Any jar that is unchipped, clean and dry. Jars should be warmed slightly in the oven beforehand to prevent them cracking when the jam is poured into them.

Jam covers can be bought in most stationers: they consist of waxed paper discs which are put on top of the jam when it is hot (they should exactly fit the surface) and parchment or cellophane circles, which are placed on top of the jar when the jam is cold and secured with an elastic band. Commercial jam jars often have screw tops which provide an airtight seal. If the metal cover is lined with a thin piece of card this should be removed and the cover washed and dried. Place a wax disc on the surface of the jam before the lid is screwed on. Plastic push-on lids are available to fit standard-sized jars and although they cost more initially they can be used time and time again. If metal or plastic lids are used they must be put on while the jam is hot – if the jam is warm, or actually cold, then mould may form.

A heat-proof jug is useful for pouring the jam into the jars, together with a long-handled wooden spoon for stirring the jam, and a slotted spoon for removing scum.

A large bowl and jelly bag or cloth are required for jelly making, although the latter may be improvised by tying a large square of cheesecloth or linen over the top of an upturned stool.

A sugar (candy) thermometer is useful if large quantities of jam are to be made as it provides the most accurate way of testing for setting or jell point.

Labels All jams, jellies and marmalades need labelling with the type of fruit and date on which it was made.

The correct assessment of setting (jelling) point is important.

Fruit

Most fruits can be used to make jams, jellies and marmalades but they must be fresh, firm, dry and slightly underripe. Over-ripe fruit will not set. Instructions for the preparation of ingredients are given in the individual recipes. After the preparation, the first stage is to soften the fruit. This must be done before adding sugar or any other ingredient. The fruit should be cooked slowly with a little water until it is soft. The amount of water and length of cooking time depends on the juiciness, ripeness and quantity of the fruit – the more fruit the less water. Soft fruits, such as blackberries, do not require any water and the softening time will be shorter.

Pectin

It is during the softening process that the pectin contained in the fruit is released. Pectin is a natural jellying substance present in most unripe fruit. When fruit becomes too ripe the pectin content alters and its setting quality becomes less effective. Fruits which are made easily into jam are those which are high in pectin, although low pectin fruits may be used successfully in conjunction with high-pectin fruits or with a pectin substitute.

High pectin fruits Citrus fruits (oranges, lemons, grapefruits, etc.); cooking apples, crabapples, cranberries, damsons, gooseberries, plums, quinces and currants.
Medium pectin fruits Apricots, blackberries, greengages, loganberries and raspberries.
Low pectin fruits Cherries, figs, grapes, pears, pineapple, rhubarb and strawberries.

Measuring pectin content

Low pectin fruits and vegetables, such as marrows (squash), will require extra acid (lemon juice or citric acid) to ensure a good set, therefore, it is advisable to measure the pectin content in the following way.

Simmer a little of the fruit until it is soft and the juice runs out. Strain off one teaspoon of the juice into a small bowl or cup. When it is cool add three teaspoons of methylated spirits (rubbing alcohol). Shake the mixture and leave it for one or two minutes. If a large, transparent, jelly-like clot forms the fruit is high in pectin; if it forms into two or three lumps the pectin content is medium; and if it breaks into small pieces the pectin content is low.

To make successful jam from low pectin fruit, extra pectin should be added and this can be done in one of the following ways:
1. Mix the low or medium pectin fruit with a high pectin one, for example, apple and blackberry.
2. Add a pectin stock made from fruits such as apples, gooseberries or redcurrants.
3. Add commercial pectin, which is available in liquid, or powdered form.
4. Add lemon juice or citric acid.
Before adding extra pectin, the fruit must be very soft. The amount of pectin to add can vary according to the fruit used but a general guide is 150ml/5fl oz ($\frac{5}{8}$ cup) pectin stock to 2kg (4lb) fruit. With commercial pectin, a short boiling method is used and more sugar is required. Follow the directions on the packet. If using lemon juice, 2 tablespoons to 2kg (4lb) fruit is generally sufficient.

Sugar

The next stage is to add the sugar. Granulated, preserving or cube sugar, made from either cane or beet, can be used.

The advantage of using preserving sugar is that less scum is formed and the jam generally has a clearer appearance. Brown sugar may be used but as it gives a dark colour it is best to keep it for something like a chunky marmalade.

The amount of sugar required depends on the pectin content of the fruit and should represent 60 per cent of the final weight of jam; therefore, if a recipe used 2$\frac{3}{4}$kg /6lb (12 cups) sugar the final yield should be about 4$\frac{1}{2}$kg (10lb) jam. The following is an approximate guide to the quantity of sugar needed for the different types of fruit:
High pectin fruits – 550-700g/1$\frac{1}{4}$-1$\frac{1}{2}$lb (2$\frac{1}{2}$-3 cups) sugar to 450g/1lb (2 cups) fruit.
Medium pectin fruits – 450g/1lb (2 cups) sugar to 450g/1lb (2 cups) fruit.
Low pectin fruits – 350g/12oz (1$\frac{1}{2}$ cups) sugar to 450g/ 1lb (2 cups) fruit.

If too much sugar is used the jam may crystallize with storing and if too little is used it may result in fermentation. However, if a less sweet jam is preferred, less sugar can be used – although it will not keep for so long and there will be a smaller yield. The jam will, however, have a much more fruity flavour.

One final note of economy: if the sugar is warmed before adding it to the fruit, it dissolves more quickly, thereby using less energy in the process.

Test for setting (jelling)

A test to see if setting point has been reached should be made after the jam, jelly or marmalade has been cooked for the time suggested in the recipe. Care should be taken not to boil beyond setting point otherwise the colour, texture and flavour will be spoiled, so the pan should always be removed from the heat during testing. Testing for setting point can be done in several ways and it is advisable to use more than one test.
1. The simplest way is to put a teaspoon of the hot mixture on a saucer and leave it to cool. When cool, the surface should be set and the jam should crinkle when pushed with a finger. If it is still runny, return the pan to the heat and continue boiling and testing until set.
2. Dip a wooden spoon into the jam, remove it and after a second or two, tilt the spoon so that the jam drips. If the drops run together in large flakes then setting point has been reached.
3. Place a sugar (candy) thermometer in a jug of hot water before and after testing. Stir the jam, then immerse the thermometer into it – do not allow the bulb to touch the bottom of the pan otherwise it may break and the whole batch would be ruined! If the temperature is between 104°C (220°F) and 107°C (222°F) the jam is at setting point.

Finishing off

When setting (jelling) point is reached, remove the pan from the heat at once and, using a slotted spoon, remove any scum from the surface. If the jam contains whole fruit, such as strawberries, or peel, as in marmalade, leave it to cool slightly until a thin skin forms on top (this prevents the fruit from rising to the top). Stir gently and pour into the warm jars. Top with a waxed paper circle or hot paraffin wax and press down gently to exclude any air. Wipe the rims of the jars if they are sticky, then cover when either hot or cold depending on the covering used. Label and store the jars in a cool, dark place.

Jams

Prepare the fruit by removing any stalks or leaves. Rinse in cold water if necessary. Fruit with stones (pits), such as cherries, peaches, plums and greengages, may be left whole or stoned (pitted), as required. The latter is preferable as it makes for easier use, particularly if the jam is to be used for tart and cake fillings. For apricot and plum jam, the stones may be cracked and the inner white kernel added to the fruit to give additional flavour.

Cook the fruit, with or without water as applicable, over low heat until it is completely softened and broken down. Add the sugar and pectin, if necessary, cook slowly and stir frequently until the sugar has dissolved. Then raise the heat and boil the jam rapidly without stirring. Take care that the jam does not rise to the top of the pan – if it does, give it a gentle stir to cool it down a fraction. Providing the initial cooking of the fruit has been sufficient the jam should reach setting point within 5 to 20 minutes.

Pour the jam into jars leaving a 12mm ($\frac{1}{2}$in) headspace, cover and label.

Dried Apricot Jam

About 2¼kg (5lb)	Metric/UK	US
Dried apricots	450g/1lb	1lb
Water	1¾l/3pts	7½ cups
Juice of 1 lemon		
Sugar	1½kg/3lb	6 cups
Blanched almonds	50g/2oz	⅓ cup

Wash the apricots and cut into pieces. Place them in a large bowl with the water, making sure they are completely covered, and set aside for 24 hours.

Transfer the apricots and water to a preserving pan or large saucepan, and simmer for 30 minutes or until the apricots are very soft. Add the lemon juice and sugar and stir until the sugar has dissolved. Add the almonds and bring the mixture to the boil. Boil rapidly for 15 minutes and test for setting point.

Put into jars, cover and label.

Apricot Jam

About 4½kg (10lb)	Metric/UK	US
Apricots	2¾kg/6lb	6lb
Water	600ml/1pt	2½ cups
Sugar	2¾kg/6lb	12 cups

Wash the fruit, cut into halves and remove the stones (pits). Place the fruit in a preserving pan or large saucepan. Split a few of the stones and remove the white kernels. Blanch these in boiling water, drain and chop, and add

them to the apricots. Add the water and cook gently until the apricots are soft. Add the sugar and stir until it has dissolved. Bring to the boil and boil for 15 minutes. Test for setting and if necessary boil again until setting point has been reached. Skim the scum off the surface of the jam with a metal spoon.

Put into jars, cover and label.

Damson Jam

About 2¼kg (5lb)	Metric/UK	US
Damsons, washed and stoned (pitted)	2kg/4lb	4lb
Water	600ml/1pt	2½ cups
Sugar	2-2¾kg/ 4-6lb	8-12 cups

Preheat the oven to cool 150°C (300°F, Gas Mark 2).

Place the damsons and water in an ovenproof dish or pan. Cover the dish or pan and place it in the oven. Leave to cook for at least 8 hours.

Remove the dish from the oven and measure the quantity of fruit and liquid. Pour the fruit and liquid into a preserving pan and add 450g/1lb (2 cups) of sugar to each 600ml/1pt (2½ cups) of the fruit and liquid.

Place the pan over moderate heat and stir until the sugar dissolves.

Increase the heat to high and boil briskly for 2 minutes or until setting point is reached. With a metal spoon, skim any scum off the surface.

Remove the pan from the heat and pour the jam into clean, dry, warmed jam jars. Cover, label and store in a cool, dry place.

Damsons and apricots, whether fresh or dried, provide the basis for three delicious jams.

Raspberry Jam

About 2¾kg (6lb)	Metric/UK	US
Raspberries, hulled and washed	2kg/4lb	4lb
Lemon juice	2tbsp	2tbsp
Sugar	2kg/4lb	8 cups

Place the raspberries in a preserving pan and cook very gently until some of the juice is extracted from the fruit. Add the lemon juice and simmer, stirring frequently, for 15 to 20 minutes until the fruit is soft. Add the sugar and stir until the sugar has dissolved.

Bring the mixture to the boil and boil rapidly, stirring frequently, for 10 minutes or until setting point is reached. With a metal spoon, skim off any scum from the surface of the jam.

Put into jars, cover and label.

Greengage Jam

About 4½kg (10lb)	Metric/UK	US
Greengages, washed, halved, and stoned (pitted)	2¾kg/6lb	6lb
Water	600ml/1pt	2½ cups
Sugar	2¾kg/6lb	12 cups

In a preserving pan or large saucepan, bring the greengages and water to the boil over high heat. Crack ten of the stones (pits) and add the kernels to the pan.

Reduce the heat to moderate and simmer for 20 minutes, or until the greengages are soft. Add the sugar and stir until it has dissolved.

Bring the jam to the boil and boil for about 15 minutes or until setting point is reached. Remove the pan from the heat. With a slotted spoon, skim off the scum from the surface of the jam.

Pour into clean, dry, warmed jam jars. Seal, label and store in a cool, dry place.

Pineapple Jam

About 2¾kg (6lb)	Metric/UK	US
Lemons	3	3
Fresh pineapple	1½kg/3lb	3lb
Water	600ml/1pt	2½ cups
Sugar	1½kg/3lb	6 cups

Squeeze the juice from the lemons and set it aside. Tie the squeezed out lemons and the pips (seeds) in a cheesecloth bag.

Place the pineapple, the reserved lemon juice, the cheesecloth bag and the water in a preserving pan or large saucepan. Bring the liquid to the boil. Reduce the heat to low, cover the pan and simmer until the pineapple pieces

RIGHT Use surplus greengages to advantage by preserving them.
LEFT Home-made jams make very acceptable presents.

are tender. Remove the cheesecloth bag, squeezing it against the side of the pan with the back of a wooden spoon to extract as much juice as possible.

Add the sugar to the pan and cook the jam, stirring constantly, until the sugar has dissolved. Then boil without stirring until setting point is reached. Remove the pan from the heat and let it stand for 5 minutes.

Ladle the jam into clean, warm dry jam jars. Cover, label and store in a cool, dark, dry place.

Marrow (Summer Squash) and Ginger Jam

About 2¾kg (6lb)	Metric/UK	US
Peeled and seeded vegetable marrow (summer squash), cut into small cubes	2kg/4lb	4lb
Juice and very thinly pared rinds of 4 lemons		
Whole cloves	3	3
Piece fresh root ginger, peeled and bruised	12mm/½in	½in
Sugar	1½kg/3lb	6 cups
Crystallized ginger, chopped	125g/4oz	⅔ cup

Put the marrow (squash) in the top part of a steamer. Half fill the bottom half with water and bring it to the boil over moderate heat. Place the top half in place, cover and steam the cubes for 20 to 25 minutes or until they are just tender.

Remove the pan from the heat. Transfer the marrow (squash) to a large mixing bowl and add the lemon juice. Put the lemon rind, cloves and bruised ginger in a muslin or cheesecloth bag and add it to the bowl. Add the sugar and mix it in thoroughly with a large spoon. Cover the bowl and leave the mixture for 24 hours.

Tip the contents of the bowl into a preserving pan or large saucepan. Put the pan over low heat and stir constantly until the sugar has dissolved. Then stir in the

crystallized ginger. Increase the heat and boil the jam until the marrow (squash) is transparent, the syrup thick and setting point is reached.

Remove the pan from the heat. With a slotted spoon, lift out and discard the muslin or cheesecloth bag. Ladle the jam into warm jars, cover, label and store in a cool place.

Peach Jam

About 2¼kg (5lb)	Metric/UK	US
Medium-sized cooking apple, chopped	1	1
Thinly pared rind of 2 lemons		
Whole cloves	2	2
Peaches, stoned (pitted) and sliced	1½kg/3lb	3lb
Water	300ml/ 10fl oz	1¼ cups
Ground allspice	1tsp	1tsp
Sugar	1½kg/3lb	6 cups

Tie the apple, lemon rind and cloves in a double piece of muslin or cheesecloth.

Place the peaches, water and muslin bag in a preserving pan. Bring the mixture to the boil, stirring continuously, then reduce the heat and simmer, stirring frequently until the peaches are just soft.

Remove the muslin bag and press it against the side of the pan with a wooden spoon to extract as much juice as possible.

Add the allspice and sugar and stir until the sugar has dissolved.

Bring the mixture to the boil and boil rapidly for 15 to 20 minutes stirring frequently until setting point is reached. Set aside for 10 minutes.

Pour into jars, cover and seal.

Cherry Jam

About 5½kg (12lb)	Metric/UK	US
Stoned (pitted) cherries, with the stones reserved	4½kg/10lb	10lb
Juice of 5 lemons		
Sugar	3¼kg/7lb	14 cups

Put the cherries and lemon juice in a large preserving pan. Put the cherry stones (pits) in a cheesecloth bag and add it

to the pan. Bring to the boil and simmer for 30 minutes, or until the cherries are tender. Remove the bag of stones (pits) from the pan and discard it.

Add the sugar to the pan and stir, over low heat, until it has dissolved. Increase the heat to moderate, bring to the boil and cook briskly until the mixture sets.

With a slotted spoon, dipped in boiling water and dried, quickly remove the scum from the surface of the jam. Allow the jam to cook in the pan until a thin skin forms on the surface. Stir gently and pour it into clean, dry, warm jars. Cover, label and store them in a cool, dry, dark place until ready to use.

Note: Cherries contain little acid and pectin and so some people find that cherry jam is difficult to make. Sour or Duke cherries are considered best, although the acid Morello cherry is also successful. Halve the lemon juice if you use the latter.

Blackberry and Apple Jam

About 4½kg (10lb)	Metric/UK	US
Blackberries	2kg/4lb	4lb
Water	300ml/ 10fl oz	1¼ cups
Cooking apples, peeled, cored and sliced	2kg/4lb	4lb
Sugar	2¾kg/6lb	12 cups

Place the blackberries and half the water in a preserving pan. Cook gently until the blackberries are soft. Cook the apples in the remaining water until they are soft then combine the two fruits. (If a smooth jam is preferred the blackberries may be strained and added to the apples in purée form.)

Add the sugar and when it has dissolved, boil the jam until setting point is reached.

Put into jars, cover and label.

Loganberry Jam

About 4½kg (10lb)	Metric/UK	US
Loganberries, washed and hulled	2¾kg/6lb	6lb
Sugar	2¾kg/6lb	12 cups

Put the fruit in a large preserving pan. Set the pan over low heat and cook, stirring frequently, until the fruit is soft.

Add the sugar and stir with a wooden spoon until it is completely dissolved. When the sugar has dissolved increase the heat to high and bring the mixture to the boil. Continue to boil for 15 to 20 minutes, or until setting point has been reached.

Skim the scum off the surface of the jam with a metal spoon. Fill clean, dry, warm jars to within 12mm (½in) of the tops. Cover, label and store in a cool, dry place.

LEFT *Serve Peach Jam with croissants and make breakfast a special occasion.* RIGHT *Cherry Jam makes a super filling for light sponge cakes and flans.*

Plum and Apple Jam

About 2¼kg (5lb)	Metric/UK	US
Plums, halved and stoned (pitted)	700g/1½lb	1½lb
Cooking apples, peeled, cored and sliced	700g/1½lb	1½lb
Lemon juice	1tbsp	1tbsp
Water	300ml/10fl oz	1¼ cups
Sugar	1½kg/3lb	6 cups

In a preserving pan or large saucepan, bring the plums, apples, lemon juice and water to the boil over high heat.

Reduce the heat to moderate and cook for 20 minutes or until the fruit is soft. Add the sugar and stir until it has dissolved. Bring the jam to the boil and boil for 15 minutes until setting point is reached.

Using a slotted spoon, skim off the scum from the surface and pour the jam into clean, dry warmed jam jars. Seal, label and store in a cool, dry place.

LEFT Plum and Apple Jam tastes as good as it looks. BELOW The inclusion of ginger in Rhubarb Jam adds a subtle spiciness. Try using it as a filling for jam roly-poly.

Rhubarb Jam

About 2¾kg (6lb)	Metric/UK	US
Rhubarb, washed, trimmed and cut into 25mm/1in pieces	2kg/4lb	4lb
Water	250ml/8fl oz	1 cup
Juice of 1 lemon		
Piece fresh root ginger, peeled and bruised	50mm/2in	2in
Sugar	1½kg/3lb	6 cups
Crystallized ginger, finely chopped	125g/4oz	⅔ cup

Place the rhubarb, water and lemon juice in a preserving pan and bring to the boil. Add the root ginger, reduce the heat and simmer, stirring frequently, until the rhubarb is soft. Remove the piece of ginger.

Add the sugar and stir until the sugar has dissolved, then add the crystallized ginger.

Bring the mixture to the boil and boil rapidly for 10 to 15 minutes until setting point is reached. With a metal spoon, remove any scum from the surface of the jam.

Pour into jars, cover and label, and store in a cool, dry place.

Strawberry Jam

About 3¼kg (7lb)	Metric/UK	US
Strawberries, hulled and washed	2¼kg/5lb	5lb
Lemon juice	125ml/ 4fl oz	½ cup
Sugar	2kg/4lb	8 cups

Place the strawberries in a preserving pan and add the lemon juice. Simmer, stirring frequently, until the strawberries are soft.

Add the sugar and stir until the sugar has dissolved. Bring the mixture to the boil and boil rapidly for 15 to 20 minutes. Test for setting. When set, leave the jam for 10 minutes before pouring into the jars. Cover and seal.

Note: If the jam is preferred with whole fruit, then small strawberries should be used and pectin stock (page 3) added instead of the lemon juice. Also use an equal quantity of sugar to fruit e.g. 2¾kg/6lb strawberries, 2¾kg/6lb (12 cups) sugar and 450ml/16fl oz (2 cups) pectin stock. Pectin stock should be added towards the end of cooking to ensure a good set.

LEFT *Apple and Ginger Jam on fresh, crusty bread makes an ideal mid-morning snack.* BELOW *Fruit used in jam-making should be firm and unblemished.* RIGHT *From left to right: Strawberry, Pineapple, Apricot and Damson Jam and Orange Marmalade.*

Apple and Ginger Jam

About 4½kg (10lb)	Metric/UK	US
Apples	3¼kg/7lb	7lb
Piece fresh root ginger, peeled and bruised	25mm/1in	1in
Thinly pared rind and juice of 3 lemons		
Water	1l/2pts	5 cups
Sugar	2¼kg/5lb	10 cups

Peel, quarter and core the apples. Tie the apple peel and cores, the ginger and lemon rind in a large piece of cheesecloth.

Place the apples, cheesecloth bag and water in a preserving pan. Bring the water to the boil, and simmer the apples for 30 minutes or until they are soft. Remove the cheesecloth bag and, with the back of a wooden spoon, press it against the side of the pan to squeeze out as much juice as possible.

Add the sugar and stir until it has dissolved. Stir in the lemon juice. Increase the heat to moderately high and bring the jam to the boil. Boil it for 15 to 20 minutes or until setting point is reached.

Remove the pan from the heat. With a slotted spoon, skim off the scum from the surface. Let the jam stand for 5 minutes. Ladle into clean jars, cover, label, and store in a cool, dry place.

Orange Curd

About 1½kg (3lb)	Metric/UK	US
Thinly pared rind and juice of 5 medium-sized, bright-skinned oranges		
Lemon juice	1tbsp	1tbsp
Orange-flower water	2tsp	2tsp
Butter, cut into small pieces	350g/12oz	1½ cups
Castor (superfine) sugar	900g/2lb	4 cups
Large eggs, well beaten	8	8

Place the orange rind and juice, lemon juice, orange-flower water, butter and sugar in a large heatproof mixing bowl and place it over a large saucepan half filled with hot water.

Set the pan over moderately low heat and cook the mixture, stirring constantly with a wooden spoon, until the butter has melted and the sugar has completely dissolved.

Using a wire whisk, rotary beater or electric mixer, beat in the eggs, a little at a time. Cook the mixture, beating constantly, for 40 to 45 minutes, or until the curd thickens.

Remove the pan from the heat. Lift the bowl out of the pan. With a slotted spoon, remove and discard the orange rind.

Ladle the curd into clean, dry jam jars. Cover, label and store in a cool, dry, dark place.

Gooseberry Curd

About 1kg (2lb)	Metric/UK	US
Gooseberries, trimmed and washed	1kg/2lb	2lb
Water	50ml/ 2fl oz	¼ cup
Butter	50g/2oz	4 tbsp
Eggs, lightly beaten	3	3
Sugar	450g/1lb	2 cups

In a large saucepan, bring the gooseberries and the water to the boil over high heat. Reduce the heat to low, cover the pan and simmer for 20 to 25 minutes or until the gooseberries are soft and mushy.

Remove the pan from the heat and push the fruit through a strainer into a medium-sized mixing bowl, pressing down on the fruit with a wooden spoon. Discard the skins left in the strainer.

In another bowl set over a pan of simmering water, melt the butter. Stir in the eggs, sugar and the gooseberry purée. Cook the mixture, stirring frequently, for 25 to 30 minutes or until it thickens.

Remove the bowl from the heat and pour the curd into clean, dry, warmed jam jars. Seal and cover as given in the instruction for jam-making.

Using tongs, carefully immerse the filled jars to within 25mm (1in) of the top in boiling water for 5 minutes to sterilize them.

Label the jars and keep them in a cool, dry place.

Figs are not the easiest of fruits to grow, and even if you manage to bring the fruits to maturity, they quickly deteriorate. As jams should be made with slightly underripe fruit, Fig Preserve is an excellent way of prolonging the enjoyment of these fruits throughout the year.

Fig Preserve

About 1½kg (3lb)	Metric/UK	US
Green figs, stalks removed	1kg/2lb	2lb
Hot water		
Sugar	1kg/2lb	4 cups
Finely grated lemon rind	1tsp	1tsp
Lemon juice	3tbsp	3tbsp

Put the figs into a large mixing bowl and pour over enough hot water to cover them completely. Leave the figs to soak for 2 to 3 minutes. Drain them in a colander and transfer them to a wooden board. With a sharp knife, chop them into small pieces.

Weigh the figs and put them into a large saucepan. Add the same amount of sugar, that is ½kg/1lb (2 cups) to every ½kg/1lb of fruit. Add the lemon rind and juice.

Place the pan over low heat and cook, stirring occasionally, for 1¾ hours or until a thick clear syrup forms. Add a little water if the mixture becomes too thick.

Remove the saucepan from the heat and allow the preserve to become completely cold before pouring it into dry, clean jam jars.

Cover, label, and store in a dry, dark, cool place.

Lemon Curd

About 1½kg (3lb)	Metric/UK	US
Butter, cut into small pieces	350g/12oz	1½ cups
Castor (superfine) sugar	900g/2lb	4 cups
Thinly pared rind and juice of 6 large lemons		
Eggs, beaten	8	8

Place all the ingredients in a heatproof bowl set over a saucepan of simmering water or in the top of a double boiler. Cook, whisking gently, until the butter has melted and the sugar has dissolved. Pour the mixture through a strainer placed over a bowl. Discard the lemon rind. Return the mixture to a clean heatproof bowl on top of the double boiler. Cook, stirring frequently, for 35 to 40 minutes or until the mixture thickens.

Pour into clean, dry, warm bottles up to the rim. Cover and label, store in a cool place.

Note: Lemon curd does not keep for as long as jams and jellies and should be used within 3-4 months.

The sour-sweet flavour of Lemon Curd gives added piquancy to tarts, cakes and lemon meringue pie.

Jellies

The difference between jelly and jam is that the fruit for jelly is cooked until very soft and then strained through a jelly bag, piece of cheesecloth or double muslin. Only the juice is then cooked with sugar.

The basic principles are the same as for jam-making, and to achieve the required consistency the same substances – pectin, acid and sugar – are needed. The low pectin fruits and vegetables – cherries, pears, strawberries and marrow (squash) – are not really suitable on their own for jelly-making, as the amount of pectin required to give a good set will disguise the flavour of the fruit. However, a mixture of high and low pectin fruit can be used.

As the yield is not as great as in jam-making, cheap or wild fruits are often used in jellies. Blackberries, sloes, elderberries, bilberries and crabapples are all suitable, the currants (red, white, black), cooking apples, gooseberries and quinces also make delicious jellies.

The fruit should be just ripe and if there are any bruised parts these should be discarded. There is no necessity to peel or remove stems, but the fruit should be washed and large fruit, such as apples and plums, should be cut into pieces.

Cooking
As in jam-making, the amount of water required depends on the variety and juiciness of the fruit. Hard fruit and fruit with tough skins – such as apples, damsons or sloes – should be covered with water and will take a longer time to cook. The fruit should be gently simmered for about 45 minutes to one hour; press it occasionally with the back of a wooden spoon. Soft fruit, such as raspberries, require no water at all and pulp in a matter of minutes.

Straining
When the fruit is really soft, pour it into the jelly bag set over a large bowl. The jelly bag, or cheesecloth, should first be scalded by pouring boiling water through it.

Hang the bag on a frame or tie the ends to the legs of an upturned chair, so that the bag hangs down the middle. Allow the juice to drain through the jelly bag and leave it for several hours or overnight until there is no liquid left to drip. Do not be tempted to push the pulp through with a spoon or squeeze the bag as this will make the juice cloudy. If there is any doubt about the amount of pectin in the juice, it can be tested in the same way as for jam page 3); but it is worth noting that if the juice is thick and sticky it is a sign that there is sufficient pectin for setting. If the pectin content is low, the pulp and juice can be re-cooked. Alternatively return the juice only to the pan and simmer it to allow some of the water to evaporate.

LEFT *Elderberries and blackberries make lovely jellies and cost nothing.* RIGHT *The quince has a high pectin content.*

Sugar
Measure the juice and pour it into a preserving pan or large saucepan and bring to the boil before adding the sugar.

The amount of sugar used depends on the pectin content of the juice. For every 600ml/1 pint (2½ cups) of juice, rich in pectin, add 450-550g/1-1¼lb (2-2½ cups) sugar and for medium pectin content add 350g/12oz (1½ cups) sugar.

After adding the sugar, cook the mixture slowly until it has dissolved, then bring it to the boil and boil rapidly for ten minutes. Remove the pan from the heat and test for setting (page 3).

Finishing, storing and yield
When setting (jell) point has been reached, remove any scum from the surface of the jelly then pour it into the prepared jars. Cover and store in the same way as for jam. It is not possible to give accurate yields in recipes for jellies as these will vary according to the ripeness and quality of the fruit, and also by the amount of pulp lost in straining. An approximate yield is 2¼kg/5lb jelly to every 1½kg/3lb (6 cups) sugar used.

Quince Jelly

About 1kg (2lb)	Metric/UK	US
Ripe quince, sliced	2kg/4lb	4lb
Water	600ml/1pt	2½ cups
Allspice berries, bruised	6	6
Lemon juice		
Sugar		

Place the quinces in a preserving pan or large saucepan with the water and allspice berries. Bring to the boil, then

Quince Jelly not only makes a delicious filling for jam turnovers but is also an excellent accompaniment to roast pork.

simmer for 40 to 50 minutes, or until the fruit is tender.

Pour the quince pulp into a jelly bag or muslin cloth. Allow the juice to drain through for at least 12 hours. Discard the pulp.

Measure the juice before returning it to the rinsed pan. Add 1 tablespoon of lemon juice and 400g/14oz (1¾ cups) of sugar to every 600ml/1 pint (2½ cups) of liquid. Place the pan over low heat and stir until the sugar has dissolved. Bring the mixture to the boil, and boil briskly, without stirring, for 10 minutes or until the jelly reaches setting point. (Quince is high in pectin so sets well.)

Skim the foam off the surface of the jelly with a metal spoon. Ladle the jelly into hot jars, leaving 12mm (½in) headspace. Cover, label and store in a cool place.

Wine Jelly

About 2¼-2¾kg (5-6lb)	Metric/UK	US
Ripe green grapes, crushed	1½kg/3lb	3lb
Dry white wine	300ml/ 10fl oz	1¼ cups
Cooking apples, sliced	700g/1½lb	1½lb
Lemon, thinly sliced	1	1
Cardamom seeds	6	6
Sugar		
Brandy	175ml/ 6fl oz	¾ cup

Place the grapes and wine in a preserving pan or large saucepan. Bring to the boil over high heat. Reduce the heat to low and simmer the fruit for 20 to 30 minutes or until it is soft and pulpy. Add the apples, lemon and cardamom seeds and continue to simmer for 20 to 30 minutes or until the apples are pulpy.

Pour the contents of the pan into a jelly bag or cloth and allow the juice to drip through the cheesecloth or bag for at least 12 hours or overnight. When the juice has completely drained through, discard the pulp. Rinse out the preserving pan or saucepan.

Measure the juice and pour it into the preserving pan or saucepan. Add 450g/1lb (2 cups) of sugar to every 600ml/1 pint (2½ cups) of juice. Place the pan over low heat and stir until the sugar has dissolved. Increase the heat to high and bring the mixture to the boil. Boil briskly, without stirring, for about 10 minutes or until the jelly has reached setting point.

Ladle the jelly into hot, clean, dry jam jars, leaving 12mm (½in) headspace. Cover, label and store in a cool, dark, dry place.

Note: This jelly is a delicious accompaniment to cold roast veal or pork.

Apple and Elderberry Jelly

About 2¼kg (5lb)	Metric/UK	US
Cooking apples	2¾kg/6lb	6lb
Elderberries	1kg/2lb	2lb
Water		
Sugar		

Wash the apples and cut into pieces. Strip the elderberries off the stems and place them with the apples in a preserving pan. Add sufficient cold water to cover the fruit. Bring the mixture to the boil then reduce the heat and simmer for about 45 minutes or until the fruit is very soft and pulpy. Mash the fruit with the back of a wooden spoon.

Strain through a scalded jelly bag or cheesecloth and leave to drain for 12 hours or until it has finished dripping. Measure the juice, return it to the clean pan, and add 450g/1lb (2 cups) sugar to each 600ml/1 pint (2½ cups) juice. When the sugar has dissolved boil rapidly until setting point is reached.

Pour into jars, cover and label.

Redcurrant Jelly

About 3¼kg (7lb)	Metric/UK	US
Redcurrants	2kg/4lb	4lb
Water	600ml/1pt	2½ cups
Sugar		

Wash the redcurrants and place in a preserving pan with the water. Bring to the boil then reduce the heat and simmer for 45 minutes to an hour until the fruit is very soft.

Mash well, with the back of a wooden spoon, and strain through a jelly bag or cheesecloth for at least 12 hours. Discard the pulp, measure the juice, return to a clean pan and bring to the boil. Reduce the heat and add 450g/1lb (2 cups) sugar to each 600ml/1 pint (2½ cups) juice. When

Redcurrant Jelly is a traditional accompaniment to roast lamb and mutton in Britain, but tastes equally good spread on hot buttered scones or toast.

against the side of the pan with the back of a wooden spoon.

Strain the sloe and apple pulp through a jelly bag or cloth for at least 12 hours or overnight. When the juice has dripped through, measure the juice and return it to the pan. Discard the pulp.

Add 450g/1lb (2 cups) of sugar to every 600ml/1 pint (2½ cups) of juice. Set the pan over low heat and cook, stirring, until the sugar has dissolved. Increase the heat to high and bring the mixture to the boil. Boil briskly, without stirring, for about 10 minutes or until the jelly has reached setting point.

Ladle the jelly into hot, clean, dry jars. Cover, label and store in a cool, dark, dry place.

Crab Apple Jelly

About 1½kg(3lb)	Metric/UK	US
Crabapples	2kg/4lb	4lb
Cold water	1-1¾l/	5-7½
	2-3pts	cups
Rind of 2 lemons		
Sugar		

Wash the crabapples and cut out any bad portions. Quarter the apples and place them, complete with peel and core, in a large saucepan. Pour enough cold water into the pan to cover the apples, then add the lemon rind. Place the pan over high heat and bring the water to the boil. Reduce the heat to moderately low and simmer for one hour or until the apples are tender and mushy.

Pour the apples and liquid into a jelly bag and leave overnight for the juice to strain into the pan. Measure the final amount of juice and pour the juice back into the pan. Add 450g/1lb (2 cups) of sugar for every 600ml/1 pint (2½ cups) of juice.

Place the pan over low heat and stir to dissolve the sugar. Increase the heat to high and bring the juice to the boil. With a metal spoon skim off any scum from the surface. Boil briskly for about 10 minutes or until setting point is reached. Remove the pan from the heat and let the jelly cool.

Pour the jelly into hot, dry jam jars and cover, label and store them in a cool, dark place.

Rosemary Jelly

About 3¼kg (7lb)	Metric/UK	US
Cooking apples, sliced	2¼kg/5lb	5lb
Water	600ml/1pt	2½ cups
Fresh rosemary leaves	4tbsp	4tbsp
Malt vinegar	250ml/	1 cup
	8fl oz	
Sugar		
Green food colouring	6 drops	6 drops

Place the apples and water in a preserving pan or large saucepan. Stir in half of the rosemary. Bring the water to the boil over high heat. Reduce the heat to low and simmer the fruit for 40 to 50 minutes or until it is soft and

the sugar has dissolved, boil rapidly until setting point is reached.

Pour into jars, cover and seal.

Note: For a thicker jelly to be used as a condiment, the fruit may be cooked with no water. After straining, add 550g/1¼lb (2½ cups) sugar to 600ml/1 pint (2½ cups) hot juice.

Sloe Jelly

About 2kg(4lb)	Metric/UK	US
Sloes, trimmed and washed	1kg/2lb	2lb
Cooking apples, cut into quarters	450g/1lb	1lb
Juice of 1 lemon		
Sugar		

Using a large needle, prick the sloes all over and place them, with the apples, in a large saucepan. Add enough cold water just to cover the fruit and add the lemon juice. Set the pan over moderate heat. Bring the mixture to the boil. Reduce the heat to low and simmer for 1 hour or until the fruit is tender. Mash the fruit occasionally pulpy. Add the vinegar and boil for 5 minutes.

Pour the apple pulp into a jelly bag or cloth and allow the juice to drain through for at least 12 hours. When the juice has completely drained through, discard the remaining pulp.

Measure the juice before returning it to the rinsed pan. Add 450g/1lb (2 cups) of sugar to every 600ml/1 pint (2½ cups) of juice. Place the pan over low heat and stir until the sugar has dissolved. Increase the heat to high and bring the mixture to the boil. Boil briskly, without stirring, for about 10 minutes or until jelly has reached setting point.

Skim the foam off the surface of the jelly with a metal spoon. Sprinkle the remaining rosemary and the green food colouring over the jelly and stir well.

Ladle the jelly into hot, clean, dry jam jars, leaving 12mm(½in) space at the top of each jar. Label and store in a cool, dark, dry place.

Note: Mint jelly can be made in the same way, substituting 5 tablespoons of fresh chopped mint leaves for the rosemary leaves. Green food colouring may be added if desired.

LEFT The flavour of Redcurrant Jelly is an excellent complement to venison. RIGHT Rosemary Jelly tastes particularly good with lamb. Try adding some to the accompanying sauce or gravy to give additional flavour and an attractive glossy appearance. BELOW Jellies do not give such a high yield as jams, so using wild fruits, such as the sloe, is far more economical.

Mulberry Jelly

About 1½kg(3lb)	Metric/UK	US
Mulberries	450g/1lb	1lb
Large cooking apple, chopped	1	1
Water	125ml/ 4fl oz	½ cup
Sugar	700-900g/ 1½-2lb	3-4 cups

In a medium-sized saucepan, bring the mulberries, apple and water to the boil over moderate heat. Cover the pan, reduce the heat to low and cook the fruit for 20 minutes or until it is soft and pulpy. Remove the pan from the heat.

Pour the fruit mixture into a jelly bag or cheesecloth and leave it to drain. Measure the quantity of juice. For each 600ml/1 pint (2½ cups) of juice you will need 450g/ 1lb (2 cups) of sugar. Add the sugar to the juice. Place the pan over moderate heat and stir until the sugar has dissolved. Increase the heat to moderately high and bring the mixture to the boil. Boil briskly, without stirring, for about 10 minutes, or until the jelly has reached setting point.

With a metal spoon, skim the scum off the surface. Ladle the jelly into hot, dry jam jars, leaving 12mm(½in) headspace. Cover, label and store them in a cool, dark, dry place.

Note: Mulberries are low in pectin, and this jelly, which contains only a small portion of apple to assist setting, has a very light set.

Pancakes filled with Mulberry Jelly make an attractive and unusual dessert.

Guava Jelly

About 1¼kg (2½lb)	Metric/UK	US
Fresh guavas, washed and quartered	2kg/4lb	4lb
Water	175ml/ 6fl oz	¾ cup
Lime juice		
Sugar		

Place the guavas in a preserving pan or large saucepan with the water. Bring to the boil over high heat. Reduce the heat and simmer the fruit for 30 minutes, or until it is quite tender, occasionally mashing the fruit against the side of the pan with a wooden spoon.

Pour the guava pulp into a jelly or cheesecloth. Allow the juice to drain through for at least 12 hours. When the juice has completely drained through the jelly bag, discard the guava pulp.

Measure the juice before returning it to the rinsed pan. Add 450g/1lb (2 cups) of sugar and 1 teaspoon of lime juice to every 600ml/1 pint (2½ cups) of liquid. Place the pan over low heat and stir to dissolve the sugar. When the sugar has completely dissolved, increase the heat to high and bring the mixture to the boil. Boil briskly, without stirring, for about 10 minutes, or until the jelly has reached setting point.

Skim the foam off the surface of the jelly with a metal

spoon. Ladle the jelly into hot, clean, dry jam jars, leaving 12mm (½in) headspace. Wipe the jars with a damp cloth. Cover, label and store them in a cool, dark, dry place.

Note: Guava jelly is delicious served with venison or roast pork.

Bramble Jelly

About 1¼kg(2½lb)	Metric/UK	US
Blackberries, washed	2kg/4lb	4lb
Water	300ml/ 10fl oz	1¼ cups
Lemon juice	2 tbsp	2tbsp
Sugar		

Place the blackberries, water and lemon juice in a preserving pan. Simmer, uncovered, for about one hour or until the fruit is soft. Mash the fruit against the side of the pan with a wooden spoon and pour the mixture into a jelly bag or cheesecloth. Leave for 24 hours or until the juice has completely drained through. Discard the blackberry pulp, measure the juice and return it to a clean pan. Bring to the boil, then reduce the heat. Add 450g/1lb (2 cups) of sugar to each 600ml/1 pint (2½ cups) of juice and when the sugar has dissolved, boil rapidly for about 10 minutes, or until setting point is reached.

Pour into jars, cover and label.

Japonica Jelly

About 3¼kg(7lb)	Metric/UK	US
Japonica fruit	1½kg/3lb	3lb
Tart cooking apples	450g/1lb	1lb
Water	2½l/4pts	5pts
Juice of 1 lemon		
Sugar		

Cut the fruit in quarters and place in a large preserving pan or saucepan. Add the water and lemon juice.

Set the pan over moderate heat. Slowly bring the mixture to the boil. Reduce the heat to low and simmer for one hour, or until the fruit is quite tender. Mash the fruit occasionally against the side of the pan with a wooden spoon.

Pour the japonica and apple pulp into a jelly bag. Allow the juice to strain for at least 12 hours. When the juice has completely strained through, measure and return it to the cleaned pan. Discard the pulp.

Add 450g/1lb (2 cups) of sugar to every 600ml/1 pint (2½ cups) of juice. Stir to dissolve the sugar over low heat. When the sugar has completely dissolved, increase the heat to high and bring the mixture to the boil. Boil briskly, without stirring, for about 10 minutes, or until the jelly has reached setting point.

Ladle the jelly into hot, clean, dry jars. Cover, label and store them in a cool, dark, dry place.

TOP *Bramble Jelly is a traditional British favourite.* RIGHT *The fruit of the japonica comes from a very attractive shrub.*

Marmalades

Marmalade is a preserve made with citrus fruits and is traditionally served with toast at breakfast. The name is said to be derived from the Portuguese word *marmalada*, a jam made with quinces.

Marmalade can be made with oranges, lemons, limes, grapefruit or tangerines, each imparting its own tangy flavour. Citrus fruit may also be mixed with other fruits – apples, pears or pineapples – to make a pleasant combination, or flavoured with ginger or other spices if wished. The best time of the year for making marmalade is during January and February when citrus fruits are at their best and the bitter Seville oranges have their short season. If you have a freezer, Seville oranges and other citrus fruits with a limited season can be frozen, allowing you to make marmalade at any time of the year.

The main difference between marmalade and jam making is that citrus fruit skin requires long slow cooking in a large amount of water to soften it before adding the sugar. However, the length of cooking time can be shortened considerably with the use of a pressure cooker.

There are two types of marmalade: thick marmalade and jelly marmalade – the yield from the latter is less than that for thick marmalade.

Thick Marmalade

The fruit must be fresh and just ripe. It should be washed and, if necessary, scrubbed with a clean brush.

There are three methods of preparing thick marmalade, but, whichever method is used, remember that the pectin content is in the pulp, white pith and pips (seeds), *not* in the peel, so it is important to add these to the fruit while cooking.

In some recipes lemon juice or citric acid is added. This is because the acid content of the fruit may be lowered owing to the high proportion of water and sugar used in making marmalade. There is no necessity to add extra acid to marmalade made with two or more fruits, or to lemon and lime marmalades.

Method 1

This is the most usual method, and the simplest.

Scrub and scald the fruit in boiling water (this makes it easier to remove the peel). Remove the peel as thinly as possible and cut into thick or thin shreds. Place the peel, acid (if used) and half the quantity of water in a preserving pan. Bring to the boil, then simmer for one-and-a-half to two hours until the peel is soft.

Meanwhile cut the fruit and pith into pieces and simmer in the remaining water in another pan for an hour and a half. Strain the mixture through a colander placed over a bowl, then discard the pips (seeds), coarse tissue and pith and add the pulp to the peel. If a thicker marmalade is

Although marmalade is traditionally eaten at breakfast, there is no reason why you can't eat it throughout the rest of the day.

required, the pulp can be pressed through a fine nylon strainer. Add the sugar and cook over low heat, stirring frequently, until the sugar dissolves. Bring to the boil and cook rapidly until setting (jell) point is reached (see page 3). Remove any scum from the top, allow the marmalade to cool slightly to prevent the peel from rising and pour into jars. Label and store as for jam making.

Method 2

Wash the fruit and cut each one in half. Squeeze out the juice and pips (seeds) and strain the juice into the preserving pan. Tie the pips and pulp in a piece of muslin or cheesecloth. Chop the peel and pith either coarsely or finely, according to preference, and add the bag of pips (seeds), peel, acid and water to the juice in the pan. Simmer for two hours or until the peel is soft. Remove and squeeze any liquid from the bag of pips into the fruit and then discard the bag. Add the sugar and cook over low heat, stirring frequently, until the sugar has dissolved. Bring the mixture to the boil and cook until setting (jell) point has been reached. Finish as in Method 1.

Method 3

Wash the fruit and put it whole into the preserving pan with the water. Cover the pan and simmer for at least two hours or until the fruit is soft and can be pierced easily with a thin metal skewer or knitting needle.

Lift the fruit out of the water and chop it coarsely – use a knife and fork as the fruit will be hot. Remove the pips (seeds) and tie them in a piece of muslin or cheesecloth and return to the cooking liquid. Boil the liquid and pips for ten minutes. Remove and discard the bag of pips after squeezing it to extract any remaining juice. Add the fruit to the pan. Add the specified amount of sugar and finish making the marmalade as in Method 1.

Jelly Marmalade

Wash the fruit and remove the peel very thinly, so that as little pith is removed as possible. Cut the peel into fine strips and tie in a piece of muslin or cheesecloth. Cut the remaining fruit and pith into pieces and place in the preserving pan with the acid and water. Simmer for two hours. Place the bag of peel in another pan with sufficient water to cover. Cover the pan and simmer for at least an hour and a half. Remove the cloth bag containing the peel and set aside. Pour the cooking water into the pulp mixture. Pour the contents of the pan into a jelly bag placed over a large bowl and leave to drain overnight. (See Jelly Making page 17). Measure the juice and pour it into the preserving pan, bring to the boil and add 450g/1lb (2 cups) of sugar to every 600ml/1 pint (2½ cups) of juice. Add acid, if required, and the reserved peel. Finish as in Marmalade Method 1.

Dundee Marmalade

About 4¼kg(9lb)	Metric/UK	US
Seville oranges, washed	1½kg/3lb	3lb
Lemons, washed	2	2
Cold water	1¾l/3pts	7½ cups
Sugar	2¾kg/6lb	12 cups

Like other home-made marmalades, Five Fruit Marmalade not only has a superior flavour to most commercial varieties, but it is also much more economical.

Prepare by method 3.

When setting (jell) point has been reached, let the marmalade stand for 10 minutes – this is to prevent the peel from rising.

Pour the marmalade into dry, warmed jars, cover and store in a cool place.

26

Five Fruit Marmalade

About 2¼kg(5lb)	Metric/UK	US
Orange	1	1
Grapefruit	1	1
Lemon	1	1
Water	1½l/2½pts	6¼ cups
Large cooking apple	1	1

	Metric/UK	US
Pear	1	1
Sugar	1½kg/3lb	6 cups

Prepare the fruit and use either method 1, 2 or 3 for cooking. Peel and dice the apple and pear before adding them to the mixture. Pour into jars, label and store in a cool, dry place.

Dark Seville Marmalade

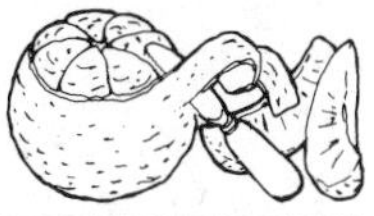

About 4½kg (10lb)	Metric/UK	US
Seville oranges	1½kg/3lb	3lb
Lemons (prepared as for oranges)	2	2
Soft dark brown sugar	2¾kg/6lb	12 cups
Black treacle or molasses	2tbsp	2 tbsp
Water	3½l/6pts	7½pts

Use either method 1, 2 or 3 for preparation and cooking. Pour into jars, label and store in a cool, dry place.

Grapefruit Marmalade

About 4½kg (10lb)	Metric/UK	US
Grapefruit	1½kg/3lb	3lb
Citric acid	2tsp	2tsp
Sugar	2¾kg/6lb	12 cups
Water	3½l/6pts	7½ pints

Use either method 1, 2 or 3 for preparation and cooking. Pour into jars, label and store in a cool, dry place.

Lime Marmalade

About 4½kg (10lb)	Metric/UK	US
Limes, washed	1½kg/3lb	3lb
Water	2l/3½pts	4½pts
Sugar	2¾kg/6lb	12 cups

Use either method 1, 2 or 3 for preparation and cooking. Pour into jars, label and store in a cool, dry place.

Lemon Marmalade

About 4½kg (10lb)	Metric/UK	US
Lemons, washed	1½kg/3lb	3lb
Water	3½l/6pts	7½ pints
Sugar	2¾kg/6lb	12 cups

Use either method 1, 2 or 3 for preparation and cooking. Pour into jars, label and store in a cool, dry place.

January and February are the best months of the year for making marmalades because citrus fruits are at their best and the bitter Seville orange enjoys its brief season. So be sure to make enough to last the whole year through.

Orange Jelly Marmalade

About 1¾kg (3½lb)	Metric/UK	US
Seville oranges	2kg/4lb	4lb
Water	4¾l/8pts	10pts
Juice of 2 lemons		
Sugar		

Prepare fruit, then cook and finish as given under Jelly Marmalade (page 25).

Brandy Marmalade

About 2kg (4lb)	Metric/UK	US
Seville oranges	1kg/2lb	2lb
Water	2½l/4pts	5pts
Juice of 2 lemons		
Preserving or granulated sugar	2kg/4lb	8 cups
Brandy	150ml/5fl oz	⅝ cup

Wash the oranges, then squeeze out the juice and pips (seeds).

Scrape the surplus pith from the orange peel, and place it, together with the pips, on a piece of cheesecloth. Tie with string into a little bag.

Cut the peel into short, thin strips, and place in a large, heavy-bottomed saucepan. Add the water, strained orange and lemon juice, and the cheesecloth bag. Simmer the original for 1½ hours or until the mixture has been reduced to approximately half the original amount.

Remove the cheesecloth bag, squeezing it well. Reduce the heat, pour the sugar into the pan and stir until it has dissolved. Add the brandy and boil rapidly until setting point is reached. This will take 15 to 25 minutes.

Remove the pan from the heat and let it stand for 15 minutes, then pour the marmalade into sterilized jars or pots and seal them.

Grapefruit Jelly Marmalade

About 1¾kg (3½lb)	Metric/UK	US
Grapefruit	1kg/2lb	2lb
1 orange and 1 lemon : total weight	450g/1lb	1lb
Water	3½l/6pts	7½pts
Sugar		

Prepare fruit, then cook and finish as given under Jelly Marmalade (page 25).

Seville Orange Marmalade

About 4½kg (10lb)	Metric/UK	US
Seville oranges	1½kg/3lb	3lb
Juice of 2 lemons		
Water	3½l/6pts	7½pts
Sugar	2¾kg/6lb	12 cups

Use either method 1, 2 or 3 for preparation and cooking. Note: 1 teaspoon of citric or tartaric acid can be substituted for the lemon juice.

Old English Marmalade

About 4½kg(10lb)	Metric/UK	US
Oranges	1½kg/3lb	3lb
Water	3½l/6pts	7½pts
Sugar	2¾kg/6lb	12 cups

Pare thinly, shred the peel, and place in a large bowl. Cut the pulp into small pieces, removing the pips (seeds), and add the pulp to the peel. Put the pips in a heatproof bowl and pour over enough boiling water to cover them. Pour the remaining water, which does not need to be boiled, over the peel and pulp and leave for 12 hours or overnight.

Pour the pips into a fine strainer and rub through the jelly, which will have formed around them. Wash any remaining jelly through with water taken from the bowl of pulp. Add this liquid to the pulp and discard the pips. Turn the pulp and peel into a preserving pan and boil until the peel is tender. Gradually add the sugar and boil until setting point is reached. Pour into jars, label and store in a cool, dry place.

The preparation of Seville Orange Marmalade is as satisfying and enjoyable as eating the end product! Jars should be stored in a cool, dry place for the best results.

Chutneys

Chutney is a condiment made from a mixture of fruits and/or vegetables which have been chopped up quite finely, cooked slowly for a long time and then preserved by the addition of vinegar, salt and spices. Although chutney is now a popular and accepted preserve throughout the world, it actually originated in India – the name being derived from the Hindu word *chatni*.

Chutney has two great advantages; it is not a seasonal preserve but may be made from fresh and dried fruits and vegetables which are available throughout the year, and secondly, unlike most other preserves, it is not essential to use perfect unblemished produce. Bruised or misshapen ingredients, provided that the bruised and damaged parts are cut out and discarded, are perfectly acceptable.

The scope of chutney is endless and the combinations and permutations can be varied according to personal taste and the ingredients available – they can be sweet, sour, hot or mild but if you are experimenting with different mixtures then it is better to make a small quantity just to be sure it is what you like!

The success of a good chutney is that it should be relatively smooth in texture and have a rich mellow flavour. To achieve this it requires long, slow cooking for about two hours then, ideally, it should be left to mature for at least two months.

Equipment

Pans should be large enough to contain all the ingredients and, if you are a keen jam-maker as well, it is well worth investing in a special preserving pan. Brass, copper or iron pans should not be used as they react with the vinegar and give a metallic flavour to the chutney.

A long-handled wooden spoon is required which should be reserved for chutney-making only. The wood becomes impregnated with the spiciness of the chutney and might taint other foods.

Heat-proof jars of any type can be used to contain the chutney. These should be clean and dry, and warmed before pouring in the chutney.

A large ladle or heat-proof jug is useful, especially when making a large quantity of chutney, to make it easier to fill the jars.

The covers are most important. Paper or jam covers should not be used as these allow the vinegar to evaporate and after a month or so the chutney will shrink and become very dry. Special vinegar-proof paper is sometimes available, usually by the roll, and this is secured to the jars by tying with a piece of string. Special preserving or bottling (canning) jars are suitable, either with screw-on or clip-on lids. Jars with tight-fitting corks may also be used, providing the corks are new. They should be boiled

By waiting until the appropriate fruits and vegetables are in season, you can greatly reduce the cost of making chutneys.

before using, then covered with a piece of grease-proof (waxed) paper and tied into the tops of the jars with string. Make sure that any metal cover is well lacquered and not scratched. To be on the safe side it is advisable to place a disc of vinegar-proof paper on top of the chutney before screwing on metal lids.

All chutneys should be labelled with the name and date then stored in a cool, dry, dark place. Providing they have been correctly covered and stored most chutneys will keep for two to three years.

Vinegar, sugar and spices

Vinegar is one of the most important ingredients in successful chutney-making, so it should be of good quality and have an acetic acid content of at least five per cent. Bottled vinegar is better than that sold from barrels. Any well-known brand of malt or distilled white vinegar is suitable, or use wine or cider vinegar for a special flavour.

As vinegar has a slightly hardening effect on some produce, particularly onions, carrots and other firm vegetables, it is advisable to cook them in water for a few minutes, then drain them, before adding to the other ingredients.

Sugar used may be granulated or brown; the latter is often used in dark-coloured chutneys. Prolonged cooking of any sugar has a darkening effect on chutney which is usually desirable. If a lighter colour is preferred then the sugar should only be added when the fruit and/or vegetables are already soft and mushy.

Ground spices are preferable to whole ones in chutney-making as they give a better flavour. If whole spices are used, double the amount given in the recipe, bruise them and tie them in a muslin or cheesecloth bag before adding to the pan. The bag is then removed before the chutney is poured into the jars.

Lemon and Mustard Seed Chutney

About 1kg (2lb)	Metric/UK	US
Lemons, washed, chopped and seeds removed	3	3
Salt	1tbsp	1tbsp
Small onions, diced	3	3
Cider vinegar	300ml/ 10fl oz	1¼ cups
Ground mixed spice or allspice	1tsp	1tsp
Mustard seed	2tbsp	2tbsp
Sugar	225g/8oz	1 cup
Raisins	50g/2oz	⅓ cup

Place the chopped lemons in a bowl and sprinkle with the salt. Cover the bowl with a clean cloth or kitchen paper towels and set aside for about 10 hours.

In a large saucepan, combine the salted lemons with the onions, vinegar, mixed spice or allspice, mustard seed, sugar and raisins.

Place the pan over high heat and bring to the boil.

Serve Date and Banana, and Tomato Chutneys with cold meat.

Reduce the heat to low, cover and simmer for 50 minutes, or until the lemons are soft.

Remove the pan from the heat. Ladle the chutney into clean, warm jam jars. Seal and label the jars and store them in a cool, dry place until ready to use.

Date and Banana Chutney

About 1½kg (3lb)	Metric/UK	US
Bananas, peeled and sliced	6	6
Medium-sized onions, chopped	4	4
Dates, stoned (pitted) and chopped	225g/8oz	1⅓ cups
Vinegar	300ml/ 10fl oz	1¼ cups

Curry powder	1tsp	1tsp
Crystallized ginger, chopped	125g/4oz	½ cup
Salt	½tsp	½tsp
Black treacle (molasses)	250ml/8fl oz	1 cup

Cook the bananas, onions, dates and vinegar in a saucepan over moderate heat for 15 minutes or until the onions are tender.

With a wooden spoon, mash the mixture to a pulp. Alternatively, put the mixture in a blender and blend for 5 seconds.

Add the curry powder, ginger, salt and treacle (molasses) to the mixture.

Cook, stirring occasionally for 15 to 20 minutes, or until the mixture is a rich brown colour.

Pour into clean, warmed jam jars. Cover, seal and label and store in a cool, dry place.

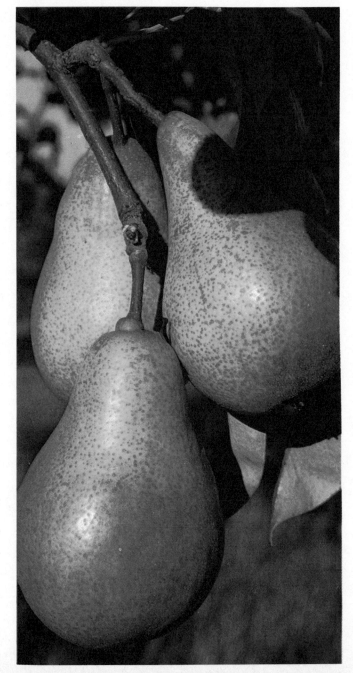

Pear Chutney

About 2kg (4lb)	Metric/UK	US
Pears, peeled, cored and chopped	1½kg/3lb	3lb
Tart apples, peeled, cored and chopped	2	2
Medium-sized onions, sliced	2	2
Raisins	450g/1lb	2⅔ cups
Chilli powder	1tsp	1tsp
Piece fresh root ginger, peeled and finely chopped	50mm/2in	2in
Garlic clove, crushed	1	1
Salt	1tsp	1tsp
Grated nutmeg	½tsp	½tsp
Cloves	12	12
Juice and grated rind of oranges	2	2
Soft brown sugar	450g/1lb	2⅔ cups
White vinegar	600ml/1pt	2½ cups

Place all the ingredients in a very large saucepan and stir well with a wooden spoon. Set the pan over high heat and bring the mixture to the boil, stirring occasionally.

Reduce the heat to low and, stirring occasionally, simmer the chutney for 3 hours or until it is thick. Remove the pan from the heat. Ladle the chutney into clean, warmed jam jars. Cover, label and store in a cool, dry place until ready for use.

Mango Chutney

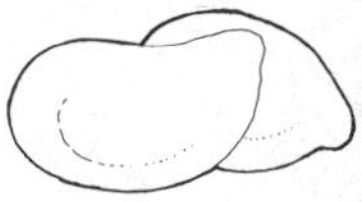

About 2kg (4lb)	Metric/UK	US
Green mangoes, peeled, halved and stoned (pitted)	1½kg/3lb	3lb
Salt	75g/3oz	⅜ cup
Water	2l/3½pts	4¼ pts
Sugar	450g/1lb	2 cups
Vinegar	600ml/1pt	2½ cups
Fresh root ginger, peeled and finely chopped	75g/3oz	⅜ cup
Cloves of garlic, crushed	6	6
Hot chilli powder	2tsp	2tsp
Cinnamon stick	1	1
Raisins	125g/4oz	⅔ cup
Stoned (pitted) dates, chopped	125g/4oz	⅔ cup

Cut the mangoes into small pieces and place in a mixing bowl, sprinkle the salt over the top and pour in the water. Cover and set aside for 24 hours.

Drain the mango pieces and set aside. Place the sugar and vinegar in a preserving pan and bring to the boil stirring frequently. When the sugar is dissolved add the remaining ingredients and bring the mixture back to the boil, stirring occasionally.

Reduce the heat and simmer the chutney for 1 to 2 hours, stirring occasionally, until it is thick; then discard the cinnamon stick. Ladle into jars, seal and label.

Pear Chutney is a tasty way of using up blemished fruit.

Green Tomato Chutney

About 2⅔kg (6lb)	Metric/UK	US
Onions, peeled and chopped	450g/1lb	1lb
Green tomatoes, peeled and sliced	2¼kg/5lb	5lb
Salt	2tsp	2tsp
Pickling spice, tied in a piece of muslin or cheesecloth	50g/2oz	¼ cup
Vinegar	600ml/1pt	2½ cups
Sugar	450g/1lb	2 cups

Boil the onions in a little water for 8 to 10 minutes or until they are soft. Drain and place in a preserving pan or large saucepan with the tomatoes, salt and pickling spices. Bring the mixture to the boil, stirring occasionally, then reduce the heat and simmer for 1 hour. Add a little of the vinegar when the mixture begins to thicken.

Stir in the remaining vinegar and the sugar, and cook, stirring frequently, for 20 to 25 minutes, or until the chutney is thick. Discard the bag of pickling spice.

Ladle into jars, seal and label and store in a cool, dry place.

Red Tomato Chutney

About 2¼kg (5lb)	Metric/UK	US
Ripe tomatoes, skinned and chopped	2kg/4lb	4lb
Dessert apples, peeled, cored and chopped	450g/1lb	1lb
Onions, peeled and very finely chopped	450g/1lb	1lb
Sultanas (golden raisins)	350g/12oz	2 cups
Raisins	350g/12oz	2 cups
Dry mustard	1tsp	1tsp
Ground allspice	2tsp	2tsp
Salt	1tbsp	1tbsp
Cayenne pepper	1tbsp	1tbsp
Soft brown sugar	700g/1½lb	4 cups
Vinegar	600ml/1pt	2½ cups

Place all the ingredients in a preserving pan or saucepan and bring to the boil. Reduce the heat and simmer for 1½ to 2 hours, stirring occasionally, until the chutney is thick.

Ladle into jars, seal and label.

Cucumber and Green Tomato Relish

About 2kg (4lb)	Metric/UK	US
Green tomatoes, skinned	1kg/2lb	2lb
Pickled cucumbers (see page 42)	1kg/2lb	2lb

(see page 42)

LEFT *Green Tomato Chutney is a perfect accompaniment to home-made curries.*

ABOVE *Serve Red Tomato Chutney with cheese and biscuits.*

	Metric/UK	US
Large onion	1	1
Red pepper, white pith removed, seeded and chopped	1	1
Salt	2tbsp	2tbsp
Ground allspice	½tsp	½tsp
Pickling spice	1tbsp	1tbsp
Dry mustard	1tsp	1tsp
Soft brown sugar	175g/6oz	1 cup
Cider vinegar	400ml/15fl oz	2 cups

Chop all the vegetables very finely. Put in layers in a large saucepan, sprinkling each layer with salt. Leave to stand overnight.

Drain off the excess moisture. Add the spice, mustard, sugar and vinegar. Boil the mixture uncovered for about half an hour, stirring frequently, until it is fairly stiff, but still moist. Pack the relish into sterilized jars, filling right to the top. Cover, seal and label.

Oriental Relish

About 2¾kg (6lb)	Metric/UK	US
Lemons	3	3
Canned, peeled tomatoes	2¼kg/5lb	5lb
Medium-sized apples, peeled, cored and coarsely chopped	10	10

	Metric/UK	US
Pieces fresh root ginger, peeled and finely chopped	4x50mm/ 2in	4x2in
Mixed spice or ground allspice	2tbsp	2tbsp
Sugar	1kg/2lb	4 cups
Soft brown sugar	450g/1lb	2⅔ cups

Cut the lemons into quarters and remove any pips (seeds). Place the lemon quarters in a blender and blend for 30 seconds. Alternatively, grate the lemon rind and chop the remaining pith and flesh very finely.

Place the blended lemons and tomatoes with the can juice, apples, ginger and mixed spice or allspice in a very large saucepan. Set the pan over high heat and bring the mixture to the boil, stirring constantly. Boil for 3 minutes. Reduce the heat to low and stir in both sugars. Simmer the mixture, stirring occasionally, for 2 to 2½ hours or until it is thick.

Remove the pan from the heat. Ladle the relish into clean, warmed jars. Cover and store in a cool dry place until ready to use.

Note: As this recipe does not include vinegar it may not keep quite as long as other chutneys or relishes.

Norfolk Fruit Chutney

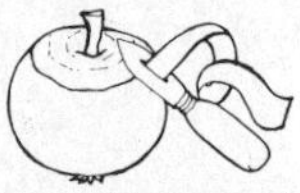

About 3¾kg (8lb)	Metric/UK	US
Apricots, halved, stoned (pitted) and chopped	1kg/2lb	2lb
Tart cooking apples, peeled, cored and chopped	1kg/2lb	2lb
Medium-sized peaches, peeled, halved, stoned (pitted) and chopped	4	4
Medium-sized onions, finely chopped	2	2
Raisins	225g/8oz	1⅓ cups
Piece fresh root ginger, peeled and finely chopped	50mm/2in	2in
Grated nutmeg	¾tsp	¾tsp
Ground allspice	¾tsp	¾tsp
Dry mustard	¾tsp	¾tsp
Finely grated rind of 1 large lemon		
Juice and finely grated rind of 2 oranges		
White wine vinegar	750ml/ 1¼pts	3 cups
Sugar	450g/1lb	2 cups
Soft brown sugar	450g/1lb	2⅔ cups

In a very large saucepan, or preserving pan, combine the apricots, apples, peaches, onions, raisins, ginger, nutmeg, allspice, mustard, lemon rind, orange juice and rind and 600ml/1 pint (2½ cups) of the vinegar.

Place the pan over moderately high heat and bring the mixture to the boil, stirring constantly. Reduce the heat to low and simmer, stirring occasionally, for 1 to 1½ hours or until the fruit mixture is very soft and pulpy.

Stir in the sugars and the remaining vinegar and simmer, stirring occasionally, for 40 to 50 minutes, or until the chutney is very thick.

Remove the pan from the heat. Ladle the chutney into clean, warm dry jars. Seal, label and store in a cool, dry dark place for 6 weeks before serving.

Rhubarb Chutney

About 2¾kg(6lb)	Metric/UK	US
Rhubarb, sliced	2¾kg/6lb	6lb
Onions, peeled and finely chopped	450g/1lb	1lb
Clove of garlic, crushed	1	1
Ground mixed spice	2tbs	2tbs
Salt	1tbsp	1tbsp
Vinegar	1l/1¾pt	4½ cups
Sugar	1kg/2lb	4 cups

Place the rhubarb, onions, garlic, spice, salt and half the vinegar in a preserving pan. Bring to the boil then reduce the heat and simmer until the rhubarb is very soft. Add sugar and remaining vinegar, and simmer, stirring frequently, until the chutney is thick.

Ladle into jars, seal and label.

Apple and Raisin Chutney

About 3¼kg (7lb)	Metric/UK	US
Cooking apples, peeled, cored and chopped	2kg/4lb	4lb

RIGHT *Home-made chutneys, like all preserves, make very pleasing gifts.* BELOW *Serve Norfolk Fruit Chutney with cheese and crusty bread for a light luncheon or supper.*

Medium-sized onions, peeled and finely chopped	4	4
Cloves of garlic, crushed	2	2
Juice of 1 lemon		
Mustard seeds	1tbsp	1tbsp
Vinegar	900ml/1½pts	3¾ cups
Raisins	450g/1lb	2⅔ cups
Ground ginger	1tbsp	1tbsp
Salt	2tsp	2tsp
Soft brown sugar	1kg/2lb	5⅓ cups

Place the apples, onions, garlic, lemon juice, mustard seeds and 600ml/1 pint (2½ cups) of the vinegar in a preserving pan. Bring to the boil then reduce the heat and simmer for 1 hour or until the mixture is soft. Add the raisins, ground ginger, salt, sugar and remaining vinegar and simmer, stirring frequently, until the chutney is thick.

Ladle into jars, seal and label.

Corn Relish

About 2kg/4lb	Metric/UK	US
Cider vinegar	1l/1¾pts	4½ cups
Sugar	225g/8oz	1 cup
Salt	1tsp	1tsp
Ground cloves	½tsp	½tsp
Dry mustard	1½tbsp	1½tbsp
Turmeric	1tsp	1tsp
White cabbage	450g/1lb	1lb
Medium-sized onions	2	2
Red peppers, white pith removed and seeded	2	2
Green peppers, white pith removed and seeded	2	2
Corn kernels, fresh, canned or frozen	1kg/2lb	2lb

Place the vinegar, sugar, salt, ground cloves, mustard and turmeric in a large saucepan and bring to the boil. Finely chop the cabbage, onions and peppers. Add them with the corn to the vinegar mixture. Simmer for an hour stirring frequently, until the mixture is fairly stiff, but still moist. Pour into sterilized jars, cover, seal and label.

Mixed Fruit Chutney

About 2kg (4lb)	Metric/UK	US
Onions, peeled and chopped	450g/1lb	1lb
Mixed fruits – apples, pears, plums, tomatoes, etc.	1½kg/3lb	3lb
Stoned (pitted) dates, chopped	125g/4oz	⅔ cup
Cloves of garlic, crushed	2	2
Salt	1tsp	1tsp
Mixed spice	1tsp	1tsp
Soft brown sugar	450g/1lb	2⅔ cups
Vinegar	600ml/1pt	2½ cups

Boil the onions in a little water until they are soft then drain off the water.

Wash, peel and core the fruits and chop into pieces. Place all the ingredients in a preserving pan, bring to the boil then reduce the heat and simmer, stirring frequently, until the chutney is thick.

Ladle into jars, seal and label.

Old Fashioned Date Chutney

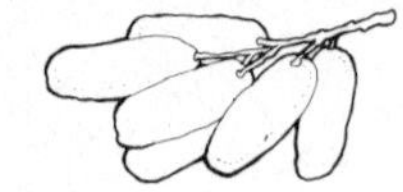

About 1kg (2lb)	Metric/UK	US
Canned, peeled tomatoes	450g/1lb	1lb
Stoned (pitted) dates	225g/8oz	1⅓ cups
Raisins	125g/4oz	⅔ cup
Currants	125g/4oz	⅔ cup
Vinegar	125ml/4fl oz	½ cup
Salt	1tsp	1tsp
Cayenne pepper	1tsp	1tsp

Combine all the ingredients in a large saucepan. Place the pan over moderate heat and bring the mixture to the boil, stirring frequently.

Reduce the heat to low and simmer the chutney, stirring occasionally, for 1 to 1½ hours or until it is thick. Taste the chutney and add more seasoning if necessary.

Remove the pan from the heat. Spoon the chutney into jars. Cover, seal and label. This chutney will not keep for more than a month.

Gooseberry Chutney

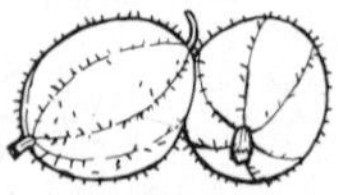

About 2¼kg (5lb)	Metric/UK	US
Onions, peeled and chopped	225g/8oz	8oz
Gooseberries, trimmed and washed	2kg/4lb	4lb
Raisins	350g/12oz	2 cups
Sugar	700g/1½lb	3 cups
Salt	1tbsp	1tbsp
Ground ginger	2tsp	2tsp
Cayenne pepper	1tsp	1tsp
Vinegar	600ml/1pt	2½ cups

Boil the onions in a little water until they are soft then drain off the water. Place the onions with the other ingredients in a preserving pan. Bring to the boil then reduce the heat and simmer, stirring frequently, until the chutney is thick. Ladle into jars, seal and label.

Serve Gooseberry Chutney with smoked fish and meats.

Pickles

A pickle is a vegetable or fruit, or a combination of vegetables and fruit, preserved in spiced vinegar. Unlike chutneys, pickles do not need to be cooked for any length of time – the exception being fruit pickles, in which the fruit is heated gently to allow the vinegar and spices to penetrate through the skin.

Vegetables used for pickling are first soaked in brine (salt and water solution) or dry salt, for up to two days. This preliminary process removes excess moisture in the vegetables, helping them to remain crisp and preventing the development of bacteria. Brine is used for most vegetables but dry salt is better for those with a high water content such as courgettes (zucchini), marrows (squash) and cucumbers.

After salting, the vegetables must be rinsed in clean, cold water and drained well before being packed into jars and bottles and covered with spiced vinegar.

Make your own supply of pickles for an instant source of varied accompaniments to cold buffet meals.

Equipment

Pickling uses the same types of pans, jars, bottles and covers as for chutney-making. (See page 29). A large bowl or bucket (not metal) is needed in addition for the preliminary soaking of vegetables.

Types of pickle

Pickles may be made from a wide variety of fruit and vegetables. As with all methods of food preservation the produce must be of good quality, fresh, firm and clean.

Large vegetables – cauliflowers, cucumbers, cabbages and marrows (squash) – are best separated or cut into pieces.

Small vegetables, such as onions (the small pickling variety), mushrooms and tomatoes, can be left whole and need only to be peeled, halved or quartered and any pips removed. Fruits that are usually pickled whole, such as damsons, plums and cherries, should be pickled before the preliminary cooking otherwise they will shrivel and dry up. Generally, the fruits that are most suitable for pickling are apples, pears, peaches and damsons – very soft fruits go mushy and are not pleasant to eat. As well as fruit and vegetables, boiled eggs may be pickled and also some nuts, particularly walnuts.

Salt, vinegar and spices

Block, coarse or sea (pure granulated) salt give better results than refined table salt: the latter may give a cloudy effect to the finished product. If brine is used to soak the vegetables an average solution is 450g/1lb (2 cups) salt to $4\frac{1}{2}$l/1 gallon (5 quarts) of water. The salt must first be dissolved in boiling water, left to cool and then strained before using. It is essential that the vegetables are completely covered with the brine. A large plate with a small weight placed on top set over the vegetables will ensure

that they do not rise and float above the liquid. If dry salt is used the vegetables should be placed in layers with a generous sprinkling of salt over each layer. Use about 1 tablespoon of salt to each 450g/1lb (2 cups) of vegetables.

Vinegar must be of good quality, and have an acetic acid content of at least five per cent. Brown malt vinegar is suitable for all pickles but if a light colour is required, particularly for light-coloured fruit and vegetables, then white malt or distilled wine or cider vinegar may be used.

Spices are added to vinegar to give it a good flavour and they also help act as a preservative. Whole spices should be used for spiced vinegar as ground ones will make the vinegar cloudy. The spices used may be varied depending on the type of pickle and on personal taste.

Recipe variations

In the following recipes there are some variations; however where only spiced vinegar is mentioned this recipe may be used: 1 stick cinnamon; 2 teaspoons cloves; 2 teaspoons allspice berries; 1 tablespoon black peppercorns; 1 tablespoon mustard seed; 2-3 bay leaves; $1\frac{1}{4}$ litres/2 pints (5 cups) vinegar. Place the spices and vinegar in a saucepan, cover and bring to the boil (do not allow the liquid to bubble). Remove the pan from the heat and set aside for two-and-a-half to three hours. Strain the vinegar and if it is not going to be used immediately pour it into clean, dry bottles.

Spiced vinegar is used either hot or cold. Usually cold vinegar is best for the vegetables that should be kept crisp – onions, cauliflower and cabbage – while hot

The same simple and inexpensive equipment can be used for making pickles and chutneys. The only additional equipment needed for pickles is a large bowl or bucket in which to soak the vegetables.

The fresh, crunchy taste of Cauliflower and Tomato Pickle goes well with cold roast turkey or pork.

vinegar gives a better result for softer fruit pickles.

Although it takes a considerably longer time, an alternative method of making spiced vinegar is to steep the spices in the unheated vinegar, in a bottle, for two to three months. The bottle should be shaken occasionally. The advantage of this method is that the full flavour of the spices really penetrates the vinegar.

Mixed pickling spice can be bought ready prepared and gives a fairly good result but preparing your own provides a wider variety of flavours.

Finishing off

All pickles should be put into jars, covered and labelled in the same way as chutneys, remembering that they must be air-tight. It is advisable to keep pickles some time before using them to allow the flavour to mature.

Pickled Red Cabbage

About 1kg (2lb)	Metric/UK	US
Red cabbage, shredded	½kg/1lb	1lb
Salt	1tbsp	1tbsp
White wine vinegar	600ml/1pt	2½ cups
Soft brown sugar	1tbsp	1tbsp
Pickling spice	1tbsp	1tbsp

Put the cabbage in a large bowl and sprinkle each layer with salt. Leave for 24 hours. Drain off any liquid and rinse off any surplus salt.

Put the vinegar, sugar and pickling spices into a pan, and bring to the boil. Simmer for 5 minutes and allow to cool for at least 2 hours. Strain.

Pack the cabbage loosely into jars and cover with the spiced vinegar. Cover with plastic lids, label and store in a cool, dark place. This cabbage can be used after a week but will begin to lose its crispness within 2 to 3 months.

As a variation a hard, round white cabbage can be pickled in the same way.

Cauliflower and Tomato Pickle

About 2¾kg (6lb)	Metric/UK	US
Medium-sized cauliflowers, separated into flowerets	2	2
Tomatoes, quartered	700g/1½lb	1½lb
Medium-sized onions, coarsely chopped	4	4
Medium-sized cucumber, coarsely chopped	1	1
Salt	175g/6oz	¾ cup
Dry mustard	1tsp	1tsp
Ground ginger	1tsp	1tsp
Black pepper	1tsp	1tsp
Soft brown sugar	225g/8oz	1⅓ cups
Pickling spice	1tsp	1tsp
White wine vinegar	600ml/1pt	2½ cups

Arrange the vegetables in layers in a large deep dish, sprinkling equal amounts of the salt over each layer. Pour over enough cold water to cover the vegetables. Cover the dish with aluminium foil and set it aside in a cool place for 24 hours.

Next day, place the vegetables in a large colander and rinse them thoroughly under cold running water to remove the excess salt. Drain off the water, shaking the colander, and place the vegetables in a large saucepan.

Sprinkle over the mustard, ginger, pepper, sugar and pickling spices. Pour over the vinegar. Set the pan over moderate heat and bring the liquid to the boil, stirring frequently.

Reduce the heat to low and simmer, stirring occasionally, for 15 to 20 minutes, or until the vegetables are tender but still firm when pierced with the point of a sharp knife.

Remove the pan from the heat. Pack the vegetables into pickling jars. Pour in enough of the cooking liquid to fill each jar. Label, cover and store them in a cool, dry, dark place.

Pickled Eggs

16 pickled eggs	Metric/UK	US
Hard-boiled eggs, shelled	16	16
White wine vinegar	1l/1¾pts	4½ cups
Green chillis (chili peppers), coarsely chopped	2	2
Ground ginger	2tsps	2tsps
Black peppercorns, crushed	2tsps	2tsps
Allspice berries, crushed	1tsp	1tsp
Mustard seed, bruised	½tsp	½tsp

Place the eggs in clean, dry preserving jars and set aside.

In a large saucepan, combine the vinegar, chillis, ginger, peppercorns, allspice berries and mustard seed. Place the pan over moderate heat and bring the vinegar to the boil. Boil the mixture for 10 minutes. Simmer for 20 minutes in a covered pan. Allow the liquid to cool in the pan and stand for 2 hours before straining. Pour the cooled liquid over the eggs so that they are completely immersed.

Seal the jars and store in a cool, dark place for at least 1 month before opening.

40

Pickled French (Green) Beans

About 2kg (4lb)	Metric/UK	US
Salt	1½tsp	1½tsp
White wine vinegar	1l/1½pts	3¾ cups
Sugar	125g/4oz	½ cup
Garlic cloves, peeled	4	4
Bay leaves	2	2
Onions, thinly sliced	2	2
Black peppercorns	6	6
Dill seed	2tsp	2tsp
Fresh French (green) beans, trimmed	1kg/2lb	2lb

In a medium-sized saucepan, combine 1 teaspoon of the salt, with the vinegar, sugar, garlic, bay leaves, onions, peppercorns and dill seed.

Place the pan over moderate heat and bring the liquid to the boil. Reduce the heat to low, cover the pan and simmer for 30 minutes.

Meanwhile, half fill another medium-sized saucepan with water and bring it to the boil over moderate heat.

Add the remaining salt and the beans and cook for 3 to 5 minutes. Remove the pan from the heat and drain the beans. Place them upright in dry, clean, preserving jars. Set aside.

Remove the vinegar mixture from the heat. Strain the mixture over the beans up to the tops of the jars. Seal the jars and store them in a cool, dark place.

Pickled Onions

About 1kg (2lb)	Metric/UK	US
Small pickling (pearl) onions	1kg/2lb	2lb
Brine	1¼l/2pts	5 cups
Sugar	50g/2oz	¼ cup
White wine vinegar	600ml/1pt	2½ cups
Allspice berries	1tsp	1tsp
Whole cloves	1tsp	1tsp
Bay leaf	1	1

Place the onions, unpeeled, in a mixing bowl and cover with brine (page 38). Set aside for 12 hours.

Drain, peel and then cover the onions with fresh brine. Leave to soak for 2 days.

Drain the onions and pack them into jars.

In a medium-sized saucepan, dissolve the sugar in the vinegar over low heat, stirring constantly. When the sugar has dissolved, add the allspice, cloves and bay leaf and bring the vinegar to the boil. Boil the mixture for 5 minutes.

Remove the pan from the heat. Cover the pan, and set it aside to cool.

When the vinegar is cool, pour it over the onions to cover them completely. Cover, seal and label the jars and store them in a cool, dry place.

Beetroot (Beet) Pickle

About 1½kg (3lb)	Metric/UK	US
Medium-sized beetroots (beets)	6	6
Cold water		
Wine vinegar	350ml/ 12fl oz	1½ cups
Dry mustard	1½tbsp	1½tbsp

Serve Beetroot (Beet) Pickle as an accompaniment to cold meats or as part of a vegetable salad.

	Metric/UK	US
Salt	½tsp	½tsp
Sugar	250g/9oz	1 cup
Onions, sliced	2	2
Dill seeds	2tsp	2tsp

Boil the beetroots (beets) until they are tender. Drain and set aside, reserving 300ml/10fl oz (1¼ cups) of the liquid. When the beetroots (beets) are cool, slice off the tops and bottoms. Then, using your fingers, slip off the skins. Slice them and set aside.

In a medium-sized saucepan bring the vinegar and reserved cooking liquid to the boil over moderate heat. Add the mustard, salt and sugar. Stir to mix, and bring to the boil again. Remove the saucepan from the heat and set aside.

Arrange the beetroot (beet) slices and onions in layers in clean, screw-top jars. Add the dill seeds. Cover with the hot vinegar mixture. Tightly screw on the tops of the jars. Cool and place in the refrigerator. Leave to stand for a few days before using. Serve very cold.
Note: Small, whole beetroots (beets) should be pickled in the same way.

Pickled Cucumbers

About 1 kg (2lb)	Metric/UK	US
Pickling cucumbers	1kg/2lb	2lb
Brine		
Spiced vinegar	1¾l/3pts	7½ cups
Dill seeds	1tbsp	1tbsp

Pickling cucumbers can vary greatly in size. If they are very large they should be sliced lengthways into con-

42

venient pieces to fit available pickling jars. Prick the skins all over so that the vinegar thoroughly penetrates them.

Place the cucumbers in a mixing bowl and cover with brine (page 38). Set aside for 3 days, drain well and pack into jars. Pour hot spiced vinegar into the jars, cover tightly and leave for 24 hours. Strain off the vinegar, bring it to the boil and then pour it over the cucumbers again. Repeat this process until the cucumbers have a good green colour. They should be completely covered with vinegar so it may be necessary to add more. Add dill seeds to the vinegar before sealing to add a piquant flavour. Cover, seal and label.

Indian Lime Pickle

About 1½kg (3lb)	Metric/UK	US
Whole limes	20	20
Green chillis (chili peppers)	20	20
Coarse rock salt	6tbsps	6tbsps
Bay leaves, crumbled	4	4
Fresh root ginger, peeled and cut into thin matchstick shapes	175g/6oz	1 cup
Lime juice	300ml/10fl oz	1¼ cups

Wash the limes in cold water and dry them with kitchen paper towels. Using a silver or stainless steel knife, make two cuts through the limes to quarter them to within 5mm (¼in) of the bottom of the fruit. Remove the pips (seeds).

Slit the green chillis lengthways and scrape out the seeds, leaving the chillis whole with their stalks.

Arrange a layer of limes on the bottom of a large pickling jar. Sprinkle with salt and crumbled bay leaves. Add 2 or 3 chillis and about 2 tablespoons of the ginger. Repeat the layering process until all the ingredients, except half of the salt, are used up. Pour in the lime juice and give the jar a good shake to settle the contents.

Cover the mouth of the jar with a clean cloth and tie it in place with string. Place the jar in a sunny place for at least 6 days, adding half a tablespoon of the remaining salt each day. Shake the jar at least twice a day. Each night, place the jar in a dry place in the kitchen. Be sure to turn the jar each day so that all sides are exposed to the sun's rays.

After the 6 days, keep the pickle on a kitchen shelf for 10 days. Cover the jar with a lid and shake the jar every day. After 10 days the pickle will be ready to eat. This is a very hot pickle, to eat with curry.

Marrow (Squash) Pickle

About 2kg (4lb)	Metric/UK	US
Large vegetable marrow, (summer squash) peeled, seeded and diced	1	1
Onions, chopped	450g/1lb	1lb
Salt	2tbsp	2tbsp
Ground ginger	2tbsp	2tbsp

	Metric/UK	US
Turmeric	2tbsp	2tbsp
Cloves	1tsp	1tsp
Green chillis (chili peppers), slit lengthways and seeds removed	4	4
Peppercorns	12	12
Soft brown sugar	350g/12oz	2 cups
Malt vinegar	2½1/4pts	5pts

In a large bowl, make layers of marrow (squash) and onions, sprinkling each layer generously with salt. Cover the bowl with a cloth and set aside for 9 hours or overnight. Drain off all excess liquid and set aside.

In a large saucepan or preserving pan, combine the ginger, turmeric, cloves, chillis, peppercorns, sugar and vinegar. Bring the mixture to the boil over high heat, stirring occasionally. Reduce the heat to low and simmer for 30 minutes.

Add the marrow (squash) and onion and stir well. Increase the heat to high and bring the mixture to the boil. Then simmer, stirring occasionally, for 1½ hours, until it is thick.

Spoon the pickle into warm jars, cover, label and store.

Spiced Cleos

About 1½kg (3lb)	Metric/UK	US
Small cleos or any fruit of the tangerine family	16	16
Bicarbonate of soda (baking soda)	½tsp	½tsp
Allspice berries	12	12
Cinnamon stick	1	1
Piece of fresh ginger root	12mm/½in	½in
Cloves	12	12
White wine vinegar	300ml/10fl oz	1¼ cups
Light brown sugar	450g/1lb	2⅔ cups

Wash the cleos and pierce a few holes in their skins with a fork. Put them in a large heavy-bottomed pan, cover with water, add the soda and boil for 12 minutes.

Place the spices on a piece of muslin or cheesecloth and tie with string to make a small bag. Add the spice bag and the vinegar to the pan, cover with a lid and simmer for 20 minutes.

Remove the spice bag and turn the heat down low. Pour in the sugar, stir until it has dissolved, then bring to the boil and simmer for a further 20 minutes, again covering the pan with a lid.

Lift the fruit from the cooking liquid with a slotted spoon and pack into a sterilized jar or jars.

Continue to simmer the liquid in the covered pan for 10 minutes more, cool slightly, then pour over the cleos and seal the jars. Store in a cool place.

Note: Spiced cleos look pretty and remain in good condition for several months providing the fruit is fully immersed in the liquid. They make an excellent and decorative accompaniment to game or pork.

The fruity flavour of Spiced Cleos is particularly suited to roast game and meat, particularly pork.

Piccalilli

About 2¾kg (6lb)	Metric/UK	US
Prepared vegetables – cucumber, cauliflower, pickling (pearl) onions, tomatoes, etc.	2¾kg/6lb	6lb
Coarse salt	450g/1lb	2 cups
Vinegar	1l/1¾pts	4½ cups
Turmeric	1tbsp	1tbsp
Dry mustard	1tbsp	1tbsp
Ground ginger	1tbsp	1tbsp
Cloves of garlic, crushed	2	2
Sugar	175g/6oz	¾ cup
Cornflour (cornstarch)	3tbsp	3tbsp

Spread the vegetables on a large dish and sprinkle with the salt. Set aside for 24 hours. Drain and rinse.

Place most of the vinegar in a preserving pan and add the spices, garlic and sugar. Bring to the boil and add the vegetables. Simmer the mixture until the vegetables are still just crisp.

Blend the cornflour (cornstarch) with the remaining vinegar and stir into the vegetable mixture. Boil for 2 to 3 minutes, stirring gently.

Spoon into jars and cover, seal and label.

Orange Pickle

About 2kg (4lb)	Metric/UK	US
Oranges	6	6
Salt	1tsp	1tsp
Sugar	450g/1lb	2 cups
Golden (light corn) syrup	2tbsp	2tbsp
Malt vinegar	175ml/6fl oz	¾ cup
Water	475ml/16fl oz	2 cups
Cardamom seeds	6	6
Black peppercorns, crushed	6	6
Ground cinnamon	½tsp	½tsp
Mixed spice or ground allspice	¼tsp	¼tsp
Cloves	12	12

Put the oranges and salt into a large saucepan. Pour over enough hot water just to cover them and place the pan over moderate heat. Bring the water to the boil, reduce the heat to low and simmer the oranges for 50 minutes or until they are tender.

Remove the pan from the heat. Drain the oranges and place them on a board to cool. In a medium-sized saucepan, bring the sugar, golden (light corn) syrup, vinegar, water, cardamom seeds, peppercorns, cinnamon, mixed spice or allspice and cloves to the boil over moderate heat, stirring constantly. Reduce the heat to low and simmer the mixture for about 10 minutes. Remove the

The hot, pungent taste of Piccalilli makes a deliciously spicy contrast to cold meat and poultry.

pan from the heat and set aside to cool.

Using a sharp knife, cut the oranges into thin slices. Pour the sugar and vinegar mixture through a strainer into a large saucepan. Discard the flavourings. Add the orange slices. Place the pan over moderate heat and bring the mixture to the boil, stirring frequently. Reduce the heat to low and simmer for 20 minutes.

Remove the pan from the heat and allow the mixture to cool for 5 minutes. Ladle the pickle into clean, warm, dry jars. Cover and label the jars and store them in a cool, dry place for at least three weeks before use. This pickle is delicious with roast goose, duck or pork.

Bread and Butter Pickle

About 1½kg (3lb)	Metric/UK	US
Medium cucumbers, sliced	4	4
Small pickling (pearl) onion, quartered	10	10
Green pepper, white pith and seeds removed and chopped	1	1
Red pepper, white pith and seeds removed and chopped	1	1
Sugar	450g/1lb	2 cups
Malt vinegar	475ml/16fl oz	2 cups
Turmeric	1tsp	1tsp
Mustard seeds	1tbsp	1tbsp
Celery seeds	1tbsp	1tbsp

Arrange the vegetables in layers in a large mixing bowl and cover with ice-cold salted water (preferably with some ice floating in it to keep the mixture cold). Cover with a plate and set aside for 3 hours. Remove the plate and drain the mixture.

Meanwhile, put the sugar, vinegar, turmeric, mustard and celery seeds in a large saucepan and bring to the boil, stirring constantly until the sugar dissolves. Add the vegetables, stir well and cover the pan. Simmer the mixture for 30 minutes, or until the vegetables are tender.

Spoon the mixture into jars, cover and seal.

Pickled Walnuts

About ½kg (1lb)	Metric/UK	US
Young green walnuts	450g/1lb	1lb
Brine		
Spiced vinegar		

Walnuts used for pickling must be young and green, and used before the hard outer skin has begun to form on them. Test by pricking with a needle and if any thin shell is felt this can be removed.

Prick the walnuts all over and place them in a mixing bowl. Cover with brine (page 38) and soak for a week. Drain the nuts and soak in fresh brine for another week. Drain well and spread out on shallow dishes. Keep in a dry airy place for 2 days until the nuts are dry and black. Pack the walnuts into jars and cover with spiced vinegar. Cover, seal and label.

Mixed Pickle

About 1½kg (3lb)	Metric/UK	US
Onions, peeled and chopped	700g/1½lb	1½lb
Cauliflower, trimmed and separated into flowerets	1	1
Cucumber, cut into cubes	1	1
French beans, trimmed and sliced	450g/1lb	1lb
Fresh red or green chillis (chili peppers)		
Spiced vinegar	1l/1¾pts	4½ cups

Place the vegetables in a large mixing bowl and cover with brine (page 38). Soak for 24 hours, drain and pack into jars, adding a chilli to each one.

Fill each jar with cold spiced vinegar, making sure there is enough vinegar to surround each piece of vegetable. Cover, seal and label.

Sweet Garlic Dills

About 3¼kg (7lb)	Metric/UK	US
Pickled dill cucumbers, sliced into thin strips	3¼kg/7lb	7lb
Sugar	1kg/2lb	4 cups
Wine vinegar	175ml/ 6fl oz	¾ cup
Garlic cloves, thinly sliced	2	2
Pickling spice	50g/2oz	¼ cup

Place the cucumber strips in a large bowl. Add the sugar, vinegar and garlic. Stir until the vinegar has dissolved the sugar to form a sticky syrup that covers the cucumber pickles. Remove and discard all but one red pepper from the pickling spice and add the spice to the mixture. Stir well, cover and leave it to stand in a cool place for 3 days.

Transfer the cucumber pickles carefully into glass jars. Strain the liquid and pour over the pickles. Cover, label and store in a cool, dry place.

Pickled Peppers

About 2kg (4lb)	Metric/UK	US
Large red peppers, white pith removed, seeded and halved	6	6
White wine vinegar	1l/1¾pts	4½ cups
Salt	½tsp	½tsp
Black peppercorns	6	6
Bouquet garni	1	1
Olive oil	4tbsps	4tbsps

Preheat the grill (broiler) to high. Place the peppers, skin sides up, on the grill (broiler) rack and grill (broil) for 5 to 8 minutes or until the skin of the peppers is black

The texture, colour and flavour of chopped Pickled Peppers make them an ideal addition to a cold rice salad.

and charred. Remove the peppers from the grill (broiler) and, with your fingertips, rub off the charred skin.

Cut the peppers into 50mm (2in) slices and pack them in sterilized preserving jars. Set aside.

In a medium-sized saucepan, combine the vinegar, salt, peppercorns and bouquet garni. Place the pan over moderate heat and bring the vinegar to the boil. Boil for 5 minutes, then remove the pan from the heat. Strain equal amounts of the vinegar into each jar and set aside, uncovered, at room temperature until it has cooled. When the vinegar is cool, pour 1 tablespoon of the olive oil on top of each jar. Cover tightly, and store.

Apple Pickle

About 1kg (2lb)	Metric/UK	US
Sugar	1kg/2lb	4 cups
Spiced vinegar	600ml/1pt	2½ cups
Cooking apples, quartered and cored	1kg/2lb	2lb

Place the sugar and vinegar in a preserving pan and heat until the sugar has dissolved. Reduce the heat and add the apples, cook until they are just tender and not broken. With a slotted spoon remove the apples and carefully pack them into jars. Boil the syrup until it reduces to 300ml/½ pint (1¼ cups) then pour over the fruit. Cover and label.

Chow-Chow

About 2kg (4lb)	Metric/UK	US
Kidney beans, soaked overnight in cold water and drained	350g/12oz	2 cups
Red or green peppers, white pith removed, seeded and sliced	4	4
Medium-sized cauliflower, separated into flowerets	1	1
French (green) beans, trimmed and sliced	450g/1lb	1lb
Frozen sweetcorn	225g/8oz	8oz
Vinegar	1l/1¾pts	4½ cups
Soft brown sugar	175g/6oz	1 cup
Dry mustard	2tbsp	2tbsp
Mustard seed	3tbsp	3tbsp
Turmeric	2tsp	2tsp

Cook the vegetables separately in boiling salted water until they are only just tender. Drain them and place in a large mixing bowl.

Place the vinegar, sugar, mustard, mustard seed and turmeric in a large saucepan. Cook gently, stirring occasionally until the sugar has dissolved, then bring the mixture to the boil. Add the vegetables and heat through for about 5 minutes.

Spoon the pickle into jars. Cover, seal and label.

Chow-chow is made from a tempting variety of vegetables.

Peach Pickle

About 2¼kg (5lb)	Metric/UK	US
Whole cloves	1tbsp	1tbsp
Allspice berries	1tbsp	1tbsp
Piece cinnamon stick	75mm/3in	3in
Piece root ginger, crushed	50mm/2in	2in
Rind of half a lemon		
Sugar	1kg/2lb	4 cups
White wine vinegar	600ml/1pt	2½ cups
Peaches, peeled, stoned (pitted) and halved or quartered, depending on size	2¼kg/5lb	5lb

Tie the cloves, allspice, cinnamon, ginger and lemon rind in a double piece of cheesecloth or muslin. Place the sugar and vinegar in a preserving pan and heat until the sugar has dissolved. Bring the syrup to the boil and boil for 5 minutes. Add the peaches and bag of spices. Simmer the peaches for about 5 minutes or until they are just soft.

With a slotted spoon remove the peaches and pack them into jars.

Boil the syrup until it has reduced by one-third. Discard the bag of spices. Pour the syrup over the peaches, allowing the syrup to penetrate through. If necessary add more syrup until the jars are full.

Cover, seal and label.

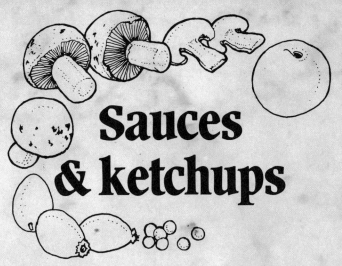

Sauces & ketchups

Sauces and ketchups are very similar things although the name 'ketchup' is actually derived from the Malaysian Kepchop meaning the brine from pickled fish. Ketchups usually have a slightly thinner consistency than sauces, and both sauces and ketchups are made from similar ingredients to those used for chutneys. The preparation and method are also generally the same, the main difference being that sauces are strained to produce a smooth purée before bottling.

The equipment for sauce-making is the same as for chutneys; however a nylon or hair strainer is essential, if a food mill or electric blender is not available. Ideally it is more practical to fill small bottles or jars as sauces and ketchups are generally used in small quantities. If large bottles are used the contents will evaporate unless used within one or two months.

Almost any type of bottle or jar may be used – commercial sauce bottles, tonic water bottles, small wine bottles, baby food jars, etc. Whichever you choose, they should be washed thoroughly and dried before use. If the tops are metal they must have a plastic coated lining and if not, a small circle of vinegar-proof paper can be placed over the bottle before the top is screwed on. If bottles without tops are used, such as uncorked wine bottles, then stop them with clean corks covered with a piece of vinegar-proof paper. If the bottles are to be processed the covers should be lightly screwed on or the corks secured with fine wire or string (this ensures they are kept in place during the heating process). When the bottles are cool, the covers should be screwed on tightly or the wire or string removed and the corks pushed firmly into the bottles. (Corks should be dry before this is done). The necks of the bottles should then be dipped into melted paraffin wax up to 12mm ($\frac{1}{2}$in) to make a complete air-tight seal.

Label the bottles with the name of the sauce and date, and store in a cool, dry place.

The addition of a sauce or ketchup made from freshly prepared ingredients to a recipe will liven up a bland dish or add a new dimension to a well-tried family favourite.

Tomato Sauce

About 1 litre/1¾ pints (4½ cups)	Metric/UK	US
Pickling (pearl) onions, or shallots, peeled and chopped	12	12
Olive oil	50ml/2fl oz	¼ cup
Fresh tomatoes, skinned and chopped	1½kg/3lb	3lb
Wine or cider vinegar	150ml/5fl oz	⅝ cup
Soft brown sugar	2tbsp	2tbsp
Salt	2tsp	2tsp
Black pepper	1tsp	1tsp

Cook the onions in the olive oil in a large saucepan until they are soft. Add the tomatoes and all the other ingredients. Bring to the boil and simmer for 15 minutes, stirring occasionally.

Turn into a blender, food mill or strainer and pureé the mixture. Check for seasoning and adjust to taste. Then pour into sterilized bottles, cover, seal and store in a cool place.

Cranberry and Orange Sauce

About 600ml/1 pint (2½ cups)	Metric/UK	US
Water	4tbsp	4tbsp
Fresh orange juice	4tbsp	4tbsp
Sugar	125g/4oz	½ cup
Fresh cranberries, washed and picked over	225g/8oz	8oz
Finely grated orange rind	1tbsp	1tbsp

Pour the water and orange juice into a medium-sized saucepan and add the sugar. Place the pan over low heat and stir with a metal spoon to dissolve the sugar. Increase the heat to moderately high and add the cranberries. Bring the liquid to the boil and cook for 5 minutes, stirring occasionally, until the cranberries are just tender and their skins begin to burst.

Remove the pan from the heat and mix in the grated orange rind. Leave the sauce to cool to room temperature. It may then be poured into glass jars and sealed with cellophane jam covers for future use. Serve with turkey or other roast meat.

Worcestershire Sauce

About 1 litre/1¾ pints (4½ cups)	Metric/UK	US
Malt vinegar	1l/1¾pts	4½ cups
Shallots, or small onion, peeled and very finely chopped or minced	4 or 1	4 or 1
Clove of garlic, crushed	1	1
Walnut ketchup	6tbsp	6tbsp
Anchovy essence	4tbsp	4tbsp
Soy sauce	4tbsp	4tbsp

Cayenne pepper	$\frac{1}{2}$tsp	$\frac{1}{2}$tsp
Black pepper	$\frac{1}{2}$tsp	$\frac{1}{2}$tsp
Salt	1tsp	1tsp

Place all the ingredients in a large bottle or jar and cover tightly. Shake the bottle or jar a few times a day for 2 weeks.

Strain the mixture into a large mixing bowl. Pour the sauce into clean, dry bottles and seal them tightly. Store in a cool, dry place.

Mustard Sauce

About 900ml/1$\frac{1}{2}$ pints (3$\frac{3}{4}$ cups)	Metric/UK	US
Green peppers	2	2
Red pepper	1	1
Green tomatoes	125g/4oz	4oz
Onions	2	2

ABOVE *Mushroom Ketchup is inexpensive and easy to make. It will keep for several weeks in air-tight bottles.* LEFT *Hot Mustard Sauce tastes good with meat, fish, poultry or eggs.*

Cucumber	$\frac{1}{2}$	$\frac{1}{2}$
Gherkins or pickled cucumbers	225g/8oz	8oz
Water	1$\frac{1}{4}$l/2pts	5 cups
Salt	1tbsp	1tbsp
White wine vinegar	600ml/1pt	2$\frac{1}{2}$ cups
Soft brown sugar	225g/8oz	1$\frac{1}{3}$ cups
Mustard seed	1tbsp	1tbsp
Flour	1tbsp	1tbsp
Turmeric	$\frac{1}{4}$tsp	$\frac{1}{4}$tsp

Remove the pith and pips from the red and green peppers, and skin the tomatoes. Roughly chop these and all the other vegetables. Place them in a large bowl, add the water and salt, and leave overnight in a cool, dry place. Next day, strain the vegetables, discarding the salt water, and place them in a large heavy-bottomed pan. Add the vinegar, sugar and mustard seed and bring to the boil.

Place the flour and turmeric in a saucer, add a drop of water and mix into a paste. Gradually stir the paste into the vegetable mixture.

Simmer the contents of the pan, uncovered, for 1$\frac{1}{4}$ hours, or until the sauce has thickened, stirring occasionally. Turn the mixture into a blender or put it through a food mill, then pour the sauce into sterilized bottles or jars, seal and label.

Mushroom Ketchup

About 1 litre/1¾ pints (4½ cups)	Metric/UK	US
Mushrooms, trimmed and wiped	1½kg/3lb	3lb
Salt	125g/4oz	½ cup
Small onion, peeled and chopped	1	1
Clove of garlic, crushed	1	1
Pickling spice, crushed	1tbsp	1tbsp
Vinegar	600ml/1pt	2½ cups

Chop the mushrooms and place in a mixing bowl. Sprinkle with the salt and set aside for 24 hours, stirring occasionally. Drain the mushrooms and rinse in cold water.

Place the mushrooms in a saucepan with the onion and garlic. Add the pickling spice and vinegar. Bring the mixture to the boil then reduce the heat, cover the pan and simmer for about 3 to 5 minutes until the mushrooms are soft. With the back of a wooden spoon push the mixture through a nylon strainer placed over a mixing bowl. Return the purée to a clean saucepan and bring to the boil.

Pour into the prepared bottles, leaving 25mm (1in) headspace, seal at once and sterilize as for Fruit Syrup (page 59).

Seal and label.

Horseradish Sauce

Horseradish roots
Distilled malt vinegar

Use fresh horseradishes and remove all the leaves. Scrape or peel the white roots, wash and dry with kitchen paper towels or a clean cloth.

Grate or shred the horseradishes into a mixing bowl. Spoon into clean, dry preserving jars or bottles, packing it down tightly. Cover with distilled malt vinegar which has been boiled for 1 minute and left until cold. Leave 12mm (½in) headspace. Seal with air-tight covers and store in a cool, dry place.

To serve: Mix a little of the horseradish with salt, pepper and mustard to taste and sufficient double cream to give a smooth consistency.

Mint Sauce

Mint leaves
Malt vinegar

Use only young, fresh mint leaves, discarding the stalks. Wash and dry the leaves with kitchen paper towels or a clean cloth. Chop the mint leaves and pack into clean, dry preserving jars.

Pour in enough malt vinegar to cover the mint, making sure the vinegar penetrates it. Leave 12mm (½in) headspace and cover with air-tight covers. Store in a cool, dry place.

To serve: Remove some mint (about 1 tablespoon per person) and add extra vinegar water, sugar and pepper to taste.

Note: An unusual and even more delicious way of serving mint sauce is to add chopped lettuce leaves and a little chopped onion to the mint sauce as well as the extra vinegar, water, sugar, salt and pepper. (Use about 3 lettuce leaves and 1 small onion to 4 tablespoons of the basic mint sauce). This version is a speciality of the Tyne and Wear areas in the North East of England and is especially good served with roast lamb or lamb chops.

The refreshing astringency of Mint Sauce makes a good contrast to mutton or lamb.

Drying herbs

Drying is one of the earliest known methods of preserving food. In prehistoric times cereals, berries, nuts and fruit were left in the sun to dry completely and then stored away for the winter months. The American Indians dried meat in the same way – it was known as pemmican. It is interesting to note that samples of dried food found on archaelogical digs at Jericho have been estimated to be 4,000 years old!

For all drying, the basic principle is the same: to remove all moisture from the food, usually by heat, thus inhibiting the growth of enzymes which cause rapid deterioration of food. As this book is designed to cover those methods of food preservation which can be carried out simply and effectively in the home, this section on drying has been restricted to herbs alone.

There is nothing quite like the taste of fresh herbs but these are not normally available throughout the year. Commercially dried herbs are freely available but they are also expensive. Therefore if you grow your own herbs, or can obtain them fresh from another source, it is well worth drying them.

The two main essentials for drying herbs at home are correct temperature and plenty of ventilation. The ideal temperature of the circulating air should be between 50°C and 65°C (120°F and 150°F). If the temperature is too high, the herbs will shrivel up. Local places for continuous drying are an airing cupboard or over a central heating boiler.

Those herbs which dry best of all are thyme and marjoram, but parsley, mint, oregano, sage, dill and fennel seeds are all worth drying.

BELOW LEFT *Herbs are well worth growing not only because of their invaluable assistance in the kitchen but also for their attractive appearance and aroma in the garden.* BELOW RIGHT *Whether you grow your own or buy them, drying fresh herbs is the best way of providing a reserve stock for the winter months. Remember that dried herbs have a stronger flavour than fresh ones and when using them in cooking the quantities recommended in recipes for fresh herbs should be halved.*

When to pick

If you are going to use the leaf, pick the herb for drying when the flowers are just in bud – the aromatic oils are then at their most pungent.

Harvest flowers just before they are fully open. Where the seeds of the herbs are used – lovage, dill, fennel and coriander – gather them when the heads turn brown. Test to see if they are ready by gently turning them upside down and shaking. If the seeds fall they are ready to pick.

Herbs, like any flowers or plants, are best picked in the early morning before the sun has reached them, but after the dew has gone – most herbs are extremely difficult to handle when wet. Use a sharp knife, and put the cut herbs into a flat basket. Avoid crushing them as they will then lose their fragrance, and do not gather more herbs than you can deal with quickly. As little time as possible must elapse between picking and drying or the aroma is lost.

How to dry

All herbs should be dried in an airy, shady place where there is no danger of condensation.

Air drying. The easiest method, when possible, is to cut sprays, tie them into bunches, and hang them upside down to dry in an airy loft or spare room – or the garage if it is not damp and there are no petrol (gasoline) fumes. They should be dry within two or three weeks. They are ready when they are brittle to the touch.

Quick-drying. The faster the method of drying the more essential basic aroma is retained, so a quick-drying method is usually preferable. Spread the herbs on newspaper, cotton, muslin or nylon stretched over a cake tray or frame. Then put them in a warm, dry place. Look at the herbs after 12 hours. Like air dried herbs they are ready when brittle to the touch. Allow them to cool thoroughly, then store them.

Storing. Strip leaves from their stems, crumble them – but not too finely or they will quickly lose their flavour – and put them into clean, air-tight containers. Some herbs such as sage, thyme and rosemary can be left on the stalk. (This makes them easier to put into casseroles and stews and remove when cooking is over.) Dried bay leaves, too, can be kept on a long stalk. They look very decorative stored in tall glass jars in a dark corner of the kitchen. Seeds and flower-heads can, of course, be put straight into a container.

If moisture starts to form on the inside of the container the herbs have not been dried correctly. Put them onto paper and allow a further drying time.

How long to keep them. Dried herbs in general last a year at the most, and the more finely powdered they are the sooner they lose their taste. It is a good idea to date your containers, so that you know exactly how long you have had the herbs. Lemon balm, parsley, summer savory and tarragon only last nine months to a year when dried. Basil, lovage, mint and marjoram last a year or more. Rosemary, sage and thyme can last longer still – but it is a good idea to replace them yearly if you can.

Note: Remember that the flavour in the leaves of herbs

A bouquet garni is a bunch of herbs, usually consisting of a sprig of parsley and thyme and a bayleaf, tied together and added to soups and casseroles to give additional flavour. Make your own instant supply of them by tying a mixture of these herbs, dried, in small squares of cheesecloth.

tends to become much more concentrated with drying so you need a much smaller amount when cooking. Usually a third to half the amount you would use fresh is sufficient.

If you are forced to rely on dried herbs a lot then keep fresh parsley going for as long as possible. Sow rows again in late summer in a sheltered spot in the garden, or put some in a pot to grow indoors. This invaluable fresh-tasting herb is a great help in bringing out the flavour of all the dried herbs.

Bouquet garni

A term frequently referred to in cooking is bouquet garni – this is a bunch of herbs – usually consisting of a bayleaf, sprig of parsley and thyme – which are tied together and used in soups and casseroles. If you are using crumbled dried herbs, and do not want bits of leaf floating in your casserole or sauce, you can tie them into a small square of muslin or cheesecloth. It is useful to prepare some of these and dry them so they are ready for instant use. The bouquet garni should be removed from the cooked dish before serving.

Herb Vinegars

These vinegars have a marvellous flavour and will improve any salad or marinade – particularly in winter when the fresh herbs are unobtainable.

Excellent vinegars can be made using the leaves of one of the following: lemon balm, basil, borage, salad burnet, dill, fennel, marjoram, summer savory, mint, tarragon – which is, perhaps the favourite – or thyme.

You can also make a mixed herb vinegar. One good one is made up of summer savory, marjoram, chives and tarragon, another from basil, rosemary, mint, tarragon and bay.

Vinegars using leaves

Use only fresh leaves to make a herb vinegar. Gather the leaves as for drying herbs (see page 53) and, in the case of the flowering herbs, just before the plants are in full bloom. You will need about the equivalent of two cups of leaves to 1¼ l/2 pints (5 cups) of vinegar.

Wash and dry the leaves and pack them loosely into a wide-mouthed glass jar. Pour in good vinegar; you can use either white or red wine vinegar, cider vinegar or malt vinegar.

It is generally held that white wine vinegar is best for tarragon, basil and salad burnet; cider vinegar for mint, and red wine vinegar for garlic.

Cover the jar tightly and put it where you will remember to shake it, or stir the contents with a wooden spoon, every other day.

After 10 days, taste it. If it is not quite herby enough take out the herb leaves, strain and start all over again.

When the vinegar is as strong as you want it, strain it into bottles through a funnel, and add a sprig of the herb to decorate the bottle.

Vinegars using seeds

You can also make vinegars from the aromatic seeds like those of coriander and dill. To make a seed vinegar you bruise the seeds in a pestle and mortar, using about two tablespoons of seeds to 1¼ l/2 pints (5 cups) of vinegar. Put them in a jar and pour on warmed vinegar. Cover the jar tightly and put it in a warm place for two weeks, shaking it from time to time. Strain the vinegar – using filter paper or cheesecloth – through a funnel into the bottles and cork tightly.

Garlic vinegar

Finally, it is worth bearing in mind that garlic, too, can be used to flavour vinegar. Put garlic cloves into the vinegar, leave them for 24 hours, and then remove and discard them.

Herb Oils

These are really extremely simple to make and they look and smell as delicious as they taste.

Experiment with different herbs, using the leaf part only. Particularly lovely herb oils can be made using basil, fennel, rosemary, tarragon and thyme. If possible make your herb oils in summer as strong sunlight is needed for the aromatic oils of the herbs to mingle with the oil itself.

Crush the herbs in a pestle with a mortar. Alternatively, put them through a blender. Then put 2 tablespoons of the crushed herbs into a 300ml/½ pint (1¼ cups) bottle. Add sunflower, corn or olive oil, filling the bottle only three-quarters full. Add one tablespoon of wine vinegar and cork the bottle tightly.

54

Put the bottle somewhere where it receives hot sunlight and leave it there for two or three weeks, shaking the bottle a couple of times a day. At the end of this time strain off the oil, and press any remaining oil out of the crushed herbs. Repeat the process – using freshly-cut herbs – until the oil is strong enough. You should be able to smell the herb quite distinctly.

If there is not enough sunshine to bring the flavour out of the herbs then put the bottles – tightly corked of course – into a double boiler and 'cook' them at just below boiling point for a few hours each day. The oil should be strong enough after seven or eight days of this treatment.

Finally, if you wish, you can for decorative purposes add a sprig of the dried herb to the bottle of oil.

Tarragon Vinegar

About 600ml/1 pint (2½ cups)	Metric/UK	US
White wine vinegar	600ml/1pt	2½ cups
Fresh tarragon, stalks and leaves bruised	50g/2oz	1 cup
Black peppercorns, crushed	4	4

Place the vinegar, tarragon and perppercorns in a crock with a cork or lid, or a wide-necked screw-topped bottle. Cover the crock or bottle and store in a cool, dry place for 2 weeks, shaking the crock or bottle occasionally.

Pour the vinegar mixture through a strainer into a jug, discarding the contents of the strainer. Pour the tarragon vinegar carefully, or through a funnel, into a warm clean dry bottle. Cork the bottle and store until required.

LEFT *Even if you do not have the use of a garden or backyard there is no reason why you cannot grow your own supply of herbs. Window boxes, ledges, roof gardens, balconies and patios are all suitable sites for their cultivation. They provide not only a source of fresh and dried herbs throughout the year but are also extremely attractive to look at. The small expenditure involved in buying seeds or small plants will be amply repaid by the time and money saved later.* ABOVE *The addition of marjoram to olive oil will not only add to its appearance but also to its taste. Although crushed herbs are used in the actual preparation, a sprig of the dried herb is normally added to the finished product for decoration.* RIGHT *In the same way that dried herbs can improve and vary the flavour of salad oils so their addition to vinegars will also vary and improve their flavour. This is particularly valuable in the preparation of salad dressings and marinades, where the quality of the ingredients has such an obvious effect on the flavour of the final dish. The vinegar illustrated is flavoured with thyme.*

Bouquets Garnis

About 8	Metric/UK	US
Bay leaves	8	8
Dried thyme	4tsp	4tsp
Dried marjoram	4tsp	4tsp
Dried parsley	4tsp	4tsp

You will need a piece of cheesecloth cut into 8 circles, each approximately 15cm (6in) in diameter.

Place a bay leaf in the centre of each piece of cheesecloth and add ½ teaspoon of each of the other herbs.

Gather the cheesecloth round the herbs to form a bag, and secure tightly with cotton or string, leaving long ends to the strings.

Store in a small, pretty container with a lid.

Tarragon Oil

About 600ml/1 pint (2½ cups)	Metric/UK	US
Fresh tarragon sprigs	4-5	4-5
Olive oil	600ml/1pt	2½ cups

Without removing the leaves from the stalks, gently bruise the tarragon by rubbing the leaves between the fingers to extract maximum aroma. Place the tarragon in a bottle, fill with oil and seal with an air-tight lid or cork. Leave to infuse for at least 1 month before using.

Variations

Mint and thyme flavoured oils can be made in exactly the same way, also basil – but the basil leaves should be strained off after 3 weeks. Herb flavoured vinegars can be made by the same method. Simply substitute an equal quantity of wine or cider vinegar for olive oil.

In addition to giving delicious extra flavour to salad dressings, herb oils and vinegar can be used in various other ways to great advantage. Suitably flavoured oils can be brushed on meat, fish, chicken and tomatoes before grilling (broiling), for example, and the use of mint vinegar when preparing mint sauce produces particularly good results.

LEFT *The parsley and sage plants in this illustration have both been successfully grown indoors. Prolong their valuable contribution to your cooking by drying them.* RIGHT *Thyme and tarragon can both be added to salad oils.*

Fruit syrups & liqueurs

It is useful to make your own supply of fruit drinks, both soft and alcoholic. Not only do they taste delicious, but they are economical and healthy. Children love the syrups and juices and it is a useful way to make sure they get essential Vitamin C. Fruit syrups differ slightly from juices in as much as the latter have some of the fruit pulp added. They are less sweet than syrups and are generally drunk undiluted. Fruit syrups are best made with soft berry fruits. Citrus fruits may also be used for syrups although they require a slightly different method of preparation. Fruit liqueurs are more extravagant as they have an alcoholic base but they are fun to make.

Fruit syrups

Huckleberries, blackberries, blackcurrants, loganberries are all ideal for making into syrups. The fruit should be fresh and ripe – in fact it is an excellent way to use fruit that is too ripe for jam making. Unripe fruit should not be used as it is too acid and the juice yield will be insufficient. Rosehips make an excellent syrup and are rich in Vitamin C. They require a slightly different method of preparation and this is given in the recipe (page 59).

Wash the fruit in cold water and drain. Place the fruit in a heatproof bowl that will fit over a large saucepan, or use a double boiler. Some fruits require a little water – blackberries and blackcurrants especially – but the minimum should be used, depending on the juiciness of the fruit. Half fill the saucepan with water and bring to the boil, reduce to simmering point. Place the bowl on top of the saucepan or the top of the double boiler over the water and heat the fruit until the juices flow out. Press the fruit with a wooden spoon while it is heating. The time taken again depends on the fruit but generally $2\frac{3}{4}$kg/6lb of fruit will take one hour. Make sure that the

water in the lower pan is replenished when necessary. When the juice is flowing freely crush it with a potato masher. When all the juice has been extracted pour it into a jelly bag with a bowl underneath it and allow the juice to drain through for 24 hours. Press the pulp thoroughly to extract any remaining juice. The amount of sugar used depends on the sweetness of the fruit but generally 350g/12oz (1½ cups) of sugar to 600ml/1 pint (2½ cups) of liquid is sufficient.

Add the sugar to the juice and stir without heating until the sugar dissolves. Strain again through muslin or cheesecloth or a fine meshed nylon strainer. Pour into clean dry bottles and cover them. Bottles with screw tops are the most convenient, but if ordinary bottles are used corks which have been boiled can be used. They will have to be secured with fine wire or string to stop them from blowing out during processing. The bottles should be filled to leave 25mm (1in) headspace for screw tops and 35mm (1½in) for corks.

Processing the bottles

Lightly seal the bottles and place them in a pan with a false bottom or rack deep enough for the water to come to the lower level of the corks. To keep the bottles upright, folds of newspaper can be put between them, but make sure the bottles are not too close together otherwise the water will not circulate freely. Bring the water up to simmering point, 88°C (190°F) and simmer for 20 minutes.

Remove the bottles and tighten the screw caps or push the corks well in as soon as possible. When the syrup is cool and the corks are dry dip the tops of the bottles into melted paraffin wax to make a completely air-tight seal. The paraffin wax should cover the screw caps or corks and come down over about 20mm(¾in) of the neck of the bottle. Label and store in a cool, dry place.

When making syrups from citrus fruits only use part of the peel, otherwise the flavour will be too strong. The rest can be finely grated or pared but none of the white pith should be used as it makes the syrup bitter and unpleasant. The juice is used with added water, more than is used for berry fruits, and the proportion of sugar is higher. Extra citric acid is usually added to these to improve the flavour but it is not essential in lemon syrups.

Bottling and processing are the same as for syrups made with berry fruits. Syrups made from citrus fruits do not keep as long, as the flavour and colour will deteriorate after about two months.

Fruit juices

The same types of fruit are suitable for juices. This is a useful way of using over-ripe fruit when there is not enough sugar available to make syrups. An average amount of sugar is 75g/3oz (⅜ cup) to each 600ml/1 pint (2½ cups) of juice.

The bottling and processing is the same as for syrups but once a bottle is opened it should be kept in the refrigerator and used within two or three days.

Note: Yield for all recipes is about 600ml/1 pint (2½ cups) of syrup or juice per 450g/1lb of fruit used, depending on the juiciness of the fruit.

Blackcurrant Syrup not only looks and tastes delicious, it is also rich in Vitamin C.

Rosehip Syrup

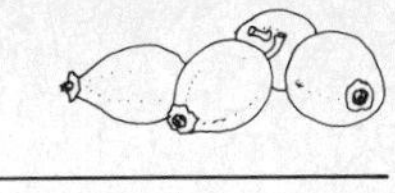

	Metric/UK	US
Water	5½l/9pts	11¼pts
Ripe rosehips	2kg/4lb	8 cups
Sugar	1kg/2lb	4 cups

Pour 3 litres/6 pints (7½ cups) of the water into an aluminium preserving pan or large saucepan. Bring to the boil.

Wash and mince (grind) the rosehips and add to the boiling water. Bring back to the boil then remove from the heat. Set aside to cool slightly for about 15 minutes.

When cooled, pour into a jelly bag placed over a large mixing bowl. (See jelly making page 17).

When the juice is drained through, return the pulp in the jelly bag to the pan and add the remaining water.

Bring the mixture back to the boil and pour into a clean jelly bag. Allow to drain until all the juice has dripped through.

Pour the two bowls of juice into a clean pan. Bring to the boil and boil until the juice reduces in quantity to about 1¾ litres/3 pints (7½ cups). Reduce the heat to low, add the sugar and simmer until it has dissolved, stirring frequently. Bring to the boil and boil for a further 5 minutes.

Pour the syrup into clean, hot bottles, cover and process as for other syrups. Once opened, rose hip syrup will not keep for more than one or two weeks so it is advisable to use small bottles.

Lemon Syrup

	Metric/UK	US
Quartered rind of 6 lemons		
Water	1l/1¾pts	4½ cups
Sugar	1½kg/3lb	6 cups
Lemon juice	600ml/1pt	2½ cups

Place the lemon rind, water and sugar in a large saucepan. Heat gently until the sugar has dissolved, stirring frequently. Strain into a mixing bowl, then add the lemon juice. Bottle and process as given on page 59.

Orange syrup is made in the same way as lemon syrup except that less sugar is required – 900g/2lb (4 cups) – and the addition of 25g/1oz (2 tablespoons) citric acid which gives extra flavour. Add the citric acid when adding the orange juice to the strained sugar and water mixture.

Blackcurrant Syrup

Blackcurrants
Water
Sugar

Wash the fruit, 'top and tail' it and them measure it. Place the fruit in a large bowl or top of a double boiler. Press with a wooden spoon to extract some of the juice. Add 300ml/10fl oz (1¼ cups) water for every 450g/1lb (2 cups) of fruit. Heat the fruit gently and continue as method on page 58.

Measure the juice and allow 350g/12oz (1½ cups) sugar to 600ml/1 pint (2½ cups) of juice.

Blackberry syrup is made in the same way but less water is required. For 2¾kg/6lb fruit, 300ml/10fl oz (1¼ cups) of water is generally required.

Raspberry or strawberry syrups: No water is required with these fruits. For the best results hull the fruit, weigh it and place in a large mixing bowl with an equal amount of sugar. Leave overnight then continue with the basic method.

Lime Juice Cordial

About 600ml/1 pint (2½ cups)	Metric/UK	US
Sugar	225g/8oz	1 cup
Water	300ml/ 10fl oz	1¼ cups
Finely pared rind of 6 limes		
Juice of 12 limes		

Place the sugar and water in a medium-sized saucepan over moderate heat. Stir constantly until the sugar has dissolved.

When the sugar has dissolved, add the lime rind. Increase the heat to high and boil the syrup for 5 minutes, then set aside to cool.

When the syrup is cool, stir in the juice of the limes and strain the cordial into a clean bottle. Cover and set aside in a cool dark place until ready for use, as a soft drink with soda and ice, or as an accompaniment to vodka or gin.

Note: This cordial should only be made in small quantities as it will only keep for a few days.

Pineapple Liqueur

About 1¾l/3pts (7½ cups)	Metric/UK	US
Fresh pineapple, peeled, cored and cut into chunks	½kg/1lb	1lb
Gin	1¼l/2pts	5 cups
Sugar	125g/4oz	½ cup
Kirsch	2tbsp	2tbsp

Put the pineapple chunks into an electric blender, a few at a time. Blend at high speed until the pineapple is completely crushed. Put the crushed pineapple into a large mixing bowl. Pour over the gin, add the sugar and kirsch and stir to blend.

Pour the mixture into a large jug or crock and cork it tightly.

Set the jug or crock aside in a warm place and allow the mixture to infuse for about 8 weeks.

Thoroughly clean and dry two bottles. Uncork the jug or crock and filter the liqueur, through a layer of fine cheesecloth, into the bottles.

Seal the bottles, and set them aside for at least 1 week before serving. The longer you leave the liqueur to mature, the better.

Blackcurrant Liqueur

About 600ml/1 pint (2½ cups)	Metric/UK	US
Cloves	6	6
Piece of cinnamon stick	50 mm/2in	2in
Blackcurrants, washed and hulled	½kg/1lb	1lb
Gin	475ml/ 16fl oz	2 cups
Sugar	75g/3oz	⅜ cup

Place the cloves and cinnamon stick in a large mixing bowl. Crush the blackcurrants and add them to the bowl. Add the blackcurrant leaves, if you are using them.

Pour over the gin and stir well to mix. Stir in the sugar, mixing until all the ingredients are well blended.

Pour the mixture into a large jug or crock and cork it tightly. Set the jug or crock aside, preferably in the sun or in a warm place, and allow the mixture to infuse for 40 days.

Sterilize and dry two or three bottles. Uncork the jug and strain the liquid through a piece of cheesecloth or muslin into a clean jug. Squeeze out any blackcurrant pulp in the cheesecloth to extract as much liquid as possible. Pour the liquid into the bottles.

Cork the bottles and set them aside for at least 5 days before serving.

Reserve your supply of home-made Pineapple Liqueur for providing a special end to a special meal.

Serve Apricot Liqueur as a welcome and refreshing change from brandy after a dinner party.

Sloe Gin

	Metric/UK	US
Sloes, trimmed and washed	½kg/1lb	1lb
Gin	1¼l/2pts	5 cups
Sugar	125g/4oz	½ cup
Almond essence (extract)	1-2 drops	1-2 drops

Using a large needle, prick the sloes all over and place them in a large mixing bowl. Pour over the gin and mix well. Add the sugar and almond essence (extract) and stir well to blend.

Pour the mixture into a large jug or crock and cork it tightly. Set the jug or crock aside in a dark place and allow the mixture to infuse for 3 months, shaking it occasionally.

Wash and thoroughly dry two bottles. Pour the mixture through a funnel lined with very fine cheesecloth into the bottles, squeezing any pulp remaining in the cheesecloth with your hands to extract the liquid. Discard the pulp.

Seal the bottles and set them aside for at least 6 months before drinking.

Note: Blackcurrant gin can be made in the same way, substituting 8 fresh or dried verbena leaves for the almond essence (extract).

Apricot Liqueur

	Metric/UK	US
Fresh apricots, halved and stones (pits) reserved	½kg/1lb	1lb
Allspice	1tsp	1tsp
Sugar	450g/1lb	2 cups
Dry white wine	900ml/ 1½pts	3¾ cups
Gin	475ml/ 16fl oz	2 cups

Place the apricots in a large saucepan and stir in the allspice, sugar and wine. Bring to the boil, stirring frequently until the sugar has dissolved. Remove from the heat and stir in the gin.

Crack the apricot stones (pits) and remove the inside kernels. Skin them and add the kernels to the apricot mixture.

Pour into a crock or jug and cover the top tightly. Set aside for 5 to 6 days to infuse.

Sterilize and dry 2 or 3 bottles.

Strain the liqueur through a piece of muslin or cheesecloth placed over a large jug or mixing bowl, squeeze as much liquid out as possible. Pour the liquid into the bottles and seal with new corks.

Allow at least 1 month for the liqueur to mature before serving. As with all home-made liqueurs the longer they are kept the better they will taste.

Pears in Brandy

About 1kg (2lb)	Metric/UK	US
Sugar	350g/12oz	1½ cups
Water	250ml/ 8fl oz	1 cup
Pears	½kg/1lb	1lb
Brandy	150ml/ 5fl oz	⅝ cup

Put the sugar and water in a heavy-bottomed pan and stir over low heat until the sugar has dissolved. Then bring to the boil and simmer for 8 minutes.

Meanwhile carefully peel the pears, keeping them whole but removing the stalks.